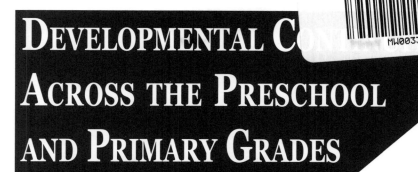

DEVELOPMENTAL CONTINUITY ACROSS THE PRESCHOOL AND PRIMARY GRADES

IMPLICATIONS FOR TEACHERS
2nd edition

Patricia A. Scully
Assistant Professor,
University of Maryland, Baltimore County

Carol Seefeldt
Professor Emerita,
University of Maryland, College Park

Nita H. Barbour
Professor Emerita,
University of Maryland, Baltimore County

ASSOCIATION FOR CHILDHOOD EDUCATION INTERNATIONAL

LB
1139.4
.B37
2003

Photographs:
p. 12, © 2003 Marilyn Nolt
p. 48, © 2003 Linda Werstiuk
p. 90, © 2003 Francis Wardle

ACEI Editors: Bruce Herzig and Anne Bauer
Production Editor: Debbie Jordan Kravitz

Library of Congress Cataloging-in-Publication Data

Scully, Patricia A., 1949-
  Developmental continuity across the preschool and primary grades :
implications for teachers / Patricia A. Scully, Carol Seefeldt, Nita
Barbour.— 2nd ed.
        p. cm.
Rev. ed. of: Developmental continuity across preschool and primary
grades / Nita H. Barbour, Carol Seefeldt. c1993.
Includes bibliographical references.
  ISBN 0-87173-161-4 (pbk.)
1. Early childhood education—Curricula—United States. 2.
Articulation (Education)—United States. I. Seefeldt, Carol. II.
Barbour, Nita. III. Barbour, Nita. Developmental continuity across
preschool and primary grades. IV. Title.

  LB1139.4.B37 2003
  372.21—dc21

                                        2003012122

CONTENTS

INTRODUCTION

Claudia, Consuela, and Laverne, friends from college who now teach different grades in two different school systems, are having dinner together. Claudia, a kindergarten teacher, exclaims: "Are you two feeling the pressure? My children are only 5 years old, but our principal is already talking about the standardized tests required in 3rd grade. You know, Laverne, our school didn't do too well on those. It seems we've all got to try some new things to get scores up. They're talking about developmental continuity, looping, multiage grouping, even forming teacher teams with the preschool programs that feed into our school. It looks like you might be next, Laverne, with your Head Start program."

"That's really interesting," replies Consuela, a 2nd-grade teacher in a neighboring district. "You know that for the past two years, we've been changing our curriculum to what we call 'developmental continuity.' We looked into those other ways of restructuring the school—like looping, where the teacher follows the same kids for two or three years. Yes, multiage grouping, too. But we decided we needed to be sure we all understood how to do a curriculum that's responsive to children's needs and developmental levels. And get this, we're going to be a pilot school for developmental continuity in our district. Our teachers are already talking with teachers from Head Start programs that feed into our schools. We're really hoping child care centers and our parent groups will join us as we move along."

"Hey, I heard about that from the Head Start Office," Laverne says. "Tell me more about it. Being in the same district, Claudia and I sometimes talk about the kids we both know, but that's not something the whole school embraces."

"Yeah, we may be faced with the same situation. Consuela, let's hear about your experiences," Claudia urges.

"Well, some of it started when we were hit with low test scores, and then at a PTA meeting a couple of years ago an irate father asked just what we 'were doing to his son.' It seems he'd sent his son to a preschool where the child chose his own activities and loved 'reading' books, telling stories, and 'writing' messages. He used play materials like blocks with letters, magnetic letters, and puzzles he could manipulate. Kindergarten the next year wasn't too bad, I guess, because the little boy could occasionally paint and make some choices after he completed his alphabet and coloring worksheets. The father's real frustration came after his son entered 1st grade—and the child began losing all interest and delight in school. The little fellow had no choices, and because he didn't do his phonics worksheets he was being made to feel he couldn't read. The father questioned why 1st grade had to be so rigid. He was seeing his son change from loving books to developing a real dislike for reading."

"How did you respond to that?" asks Claudia.

"Of course, there were different reactions and lots of dialogue, but eventually most of us began to realize that kids ought not to have to adjust to major changes as they move from home to preschool to regular school experiences. In the past we just assumed that kids coming into our classrooms were ready for our curriculum. However, that is not always the case. Well, we started to think that changes needed to be made all along the way, for us as well as for them. We really are sincere about changing our curriculum. Most of us want to provide smoother transitions and continuity of curriculum for the children from preschool through the primary grades. We have even started to include the child care and Head Start directors and some of their teachers in this planning."

"But do you think it's working?" asks Laverne.

"We're really enthusiastic about the changes we've made," Consuela replies. "Throughout this pilot year, we've spent a lot of time working with the teachers who had our kids last year and those who will have them next year. We're realizing how much more all of us can do with these children when we know them better. At this point, some of us are considering working with the same group over a longer period of time— you know, the looping idea. But before we do that, we've got to implement meaningful curriculum for all children in our regular classrooms."

"I can understand how knowing the kids better is helpful," challenges Claudia, "but how do you manage—in a classroom of 25 kids—to meet each child's needs, have various reading groups, and worry about the tests? Because the 1st-grade teacher next to me has 'the top group,' the principal expects her to have most of her 1st-graders reading at a 2nd- or 3rd-grade level by the end of the year. She freaks out, and she's pressuring me to do more to get the kids 'ready'! How do you see developmental continuity figuring into that kind of thinking?"

"Well, I'm not sure the notion of reading groups is very compatible with developmental continuity," Consuela answers. "Before we became involved in developmental continuity at my school, some of us had been trying to change our reading instruction. We wanted to be more congruent with a balanced reading program and an emergent literacy philosophy. Now, I'm finding that I think differently about how children learn to read. Not only has my classroom instruction become more flexible, but I'm learning more about each child's interests and learning processes. Did you know that a child may belong to more than one reading group at a time? And we're developing literacy centers where children can practice their new skills by themselves or with a partner. With this scheme, I'm finding more time for each individual child."

"How does that flexibility tie in with developmental continuity, Consuela?" asks Laverne. "Maybe if you gave us an example, it would help."

"I'm not sure where to begin," replies Consuela, "because I find that I use so many different strategies. Remember how we used to think that the language experience approach (LEA) to reading and the subsequent whole language approach was such a wonderful way to start the teaching of reading? Now, I have a much broader concept of what those methods were all about. Those who helped me understand a balanced approach to reading really expanded my knowledge about how children learn to read and write. What is really exciting for me now, however, is that I teach much more of an integrated curriculum, which allows my children to acquire concepts and develop needed skills at their own level of development."

"That still doesn't tell me what you do," persists Claudia.

"You're right," Consuela concedes. "In my 2nd-grade class, we discuss at least one science or social studies 'topic' each day, and we can stay on that topic for several days. For example, last week we were talking about what animals make good pets, and why. The children read a variety of materials about that topic, and then they wrote and, in some graphic way, expressed what they got from their reading. Typically, we make all sorts of lists: concepts we have learned, new words we have discovered, rules for an area of the classroom, directions for making things. Sometimes we read as a total group; usually poetry or some dramatic presentation. The children read to each other and talk about their reading. They also read to me, and of course they read silently. Writing has become a way of life for both the children and me. Journals, books, and lists are just the beginning. You know, I find doing things this way allows me to work more with kids individually, and I'm a lot more knowledgeable about their developmental needs."

"How does that fit in with the reading materials your district requires?" asks Laverne.

"Oh, I use reading anthologies and, would you believe, I've found some old basal readers that actually have interesting stories that are pertinent, and age appropriate," Consuela says. She continues, "The children are getting good at finding materials relating to the topics that interest them. And a few even check out things on the 'net! They share a lot of the stories they like, even from the old basal readers."

"Claudia, that reminds me," chimes in Laverne. "I have some children who think they can read, because they've memorized the books. They know some letters and they even recognize some words. If we spent our time together sharing how we see children learning the different aspects of reading and writing, we three would get a head start on solving these issues."

"You're probably right, and Consuela does sound excited about it," Claudia admits. "But still, the 1st-grade teacher and my principal pressure me to use more beginning phonics."

"Make no mistake," Consuela says. "I teach plenty of phonics, but I teach those phonic skills that kids need when they're writing or trying to figure out a new word in their reading. I even have developed some centers where children can find materials to help them practice their 'new skills.' And I didn't get there overnight! It took time and experimentation. I'm sure that you both do things now that support children's learning, like letter identification, beginning sounds, rhyming words, and so on. Of course, my principal is very interested in having us all know more about developmental continuity. You know, she was the first one in the district to encourage us to go to workshops that support developmental continuity. She is encouraging us to experiment with some of the techniques others have tried, too. She hired substitutes for me, so I could visit teachers who were successful in changing their curriculum. And when I began experimenting, these same teachers welcomed my questions—one even came to my classroom to observe and give me some feedback. Another teacher in the school became involved when I did, and we're supporting one another. We may even start a teacher study group. Really, the principal makes us feel that she has been learning along with us.

"Our principal does believe in keeping up with change," Consuela continues. "Because of changes in our neighborhood, the children in our school enter kindergarten with an even greater variety of educational experiences than in former years. Many have attended the Head Start program or the child care centers in the neighborhood, but several have had no preschool experiences—and there are even a few children coming from the homeless shelter. The principal called the directors of the Head Start and child care programs and invited them to start working with us. First, the directors and principal just visited back and forth. Then, we began the tradition of bringing the children to visit the 'big school' before actual entrance; and now we all attend training sessions together. All of us are beginning to understand better what these kids at different stages need to learn in order to work productively together and to initiate their own learning.

"You know, Claudia, I could help you and Laverne work together to see what changes would help you," Consuela suggests. "You might be able to convince a 1st-grade teacher to at least join in some of your efforts. Why don't you try it? We've always tried to support one another. Try some of the ideas this year, and I'll help you."

"Gee, I don't know," Claudia says. "Maybe I could try. I should ask my principal if he'd support me if I tried some of this. You know, I could start small—maybe by trying to expand my understanding of the differences between LEA, whole language, and a balanced approach to emergent literacy. I used to do more of what I thought was whole language, and I really did enjoy it. Then I felt so pressured to use all these worksheets. I suppose in some ways the worksheets make it easier on me, but the kids aren't as active or interested. Laverne, do you think we might try coordinating our curriculum as a start?"

"No harm trying," Laverne responds. "I'm really eager to help children get more experiences with books and writing, while staying within the framework of an active, play-rich environment."

Can Claudia and Laverne be successful in implementing curriculum that responds to children's developmental progress in their Head Start and kindergarten programs?

It depends.

Success will depend on their own commitment to developing educational experiences that match children's development, and also on the support they receive from the school system and their administrators. Even if the two are successful, the continued success of children will depend on something else—whether or not all of their teachers across the preschool and primary grades can work together to create continuity in their early educational experiences.

Developmental Continuity Across Preschool and Primary Years: Implications for Teachers continues to be a resource for teachers as they work together to provide experiences that respond to children's developmental progress from preschool through primary grades. This second edition recognizes that many reform programs have been tried over the years and many have floundered or merged with others. Many new programs have principles similar to developmental continuity, and many promote good practices that help children make important transitions. The basic premises remain the same. The task of providing a curriculum that meets the needs of all children never ceases. In recognition of this constant, this book suggests ways that teachers can become more skilled at educating all children.

Chapter 1 discusses the meaning of developmental continuity and its history, and Chapter 2 offers suggestions for beginning the change process. Because developmental continuity is difficult to implement without making changes in the organization of schools and ensuring coordination among preschool, kindergartens, and primary grades, making changes in the *structure* of schools also is necessary. These requisite changes are described in Chapter 3. Chapter 4 describes the creation of curriculum that responds to children's development, while Chapter 5 gives suggestions for structuring the environment in which that curriculum will be implemented. Finally, Chapter 6 examines evaluation issues and discusses methods for documenting children's progress and achievement. Together, these six chapters provide readers with an action plan for putting the principles of developmental continuity into practice.

CHAPTER 1

DEVELOPMENTAL CONTINUITY:
ITS MEANING

"Consuela, last week you talked about developmental continuity, looping, multiage grouping, and integrated curriculum. It was all about what you're doing to provide for your kids' developmental progress," persists Claudia when next she met with her two friends. "But, you know, I still don't know what developmental continuity means."

"Developmental continuity" is used to describe ways of designing early childhood instruction. Looping, multiage grouping, even integrated curriculum all are based on this underlying principle, despite their different formats. These arrangements provide teachers with tools to ensure that children have continuity in their learning. Basically, the curriculum in developmental continuity is designed to provide 1) learning experiences that are linked to children's prior knowledge, 2) experiences that flow in a natural progression across preschool and primary grades toward more sophisticated and complex content, and 3) experiences that permit progress according to each child's rate and style of learning. Increasingly sophisticated, abstract, and complex practices are possible as children acquire knowledge, learn skills, and develop positive attitudes towards learning.

To achieve this continuity, teachers need a good understanding of child development from the early years to age 8, as well as a firm grasp of appropriate content. More than that, teachers also need the support of other teachers, parents, and the community. Children's previous teachers can offer valuable insights into children's abilities and accomplishments. Teachers can use these insights to extend a child's prior knowledge and stimulate achievement. Likewise, if teachers work with parents, respecting and building on children's home learning and cultures, they will be better able to maximize children's learning. With good administrative and community support, the teacher is able to help children in his classroom succeed; all too often, however, such success does not continue when it is not supported by the home or by other school environments.

Developmental continuity can be provided in different ways. Common to all methods is the idea that teachers, parents, and administrators must work together to provide a continuum of developmentally appropriate educational experiences. Providing developmentally appropriate experiences involves:

- Basing curriculum and educational decisions on each child's social, emotional, physical, and intellectual development, as well as on the child's prior knowledge and home learning environment
- Adjusting teaching and schooling so that all children experience success and demonstrate progress in academic achievement appropriate to their individual learning styles
- Eliminating artificial barriers, such as grade or group placement according to achievement tests, that negate continuity of achievement and progress as children move from home to preschool to the kindergarten and through the primary grades
- Planning curriculum that provides a spiral of knowledge, skills, and experiences from home to preschool through the primary grades
- Developing a continuum of goals and objectives that meets community expectations, yet remains related to children's stages of development
- Ensuring smooth transitions for children as they move from home to their formal school experiences.

DEVELOPMENT IS CONTINUOUS

Children's development is continuous, sequential, and hierarchical. While children's social, emotional, physical, or cognitive growth and development may be uneven—one domain of development may spurt ahead of another—different areas of children's development cannot be viewed separately. Their "mental growth is inseparable from physical growth, . . . [and] it is widely accepted that cognitive and affective or social development are inseparable and parallel" (Piaget & Inhelder, 1969, p. vii, p. 117).

Just as children's development is continuous, so is their learning. The research of Jean Piaget, which forever changed our thinking of how children think and learn, clearly illustrated the results of children's different stages of development. He also demonstrated that certain kinds of learning depend upon inherited traits, level of maturation, and the child's experiences with the social, physical, and intellectual environments. Current brain research and genetic studies do indicate some variation in Piaget's results, but his paradigm remains a good and proven basis from which to understand developmental continuity.

Experts, interpreting brain research results, contend that "a baby does not come into the world as a genetically programmed automaton or a blank slate at the mercy of the environment" (Nash, 1997). Growth and learning is a complex process, and brain research supports Piaget's theory that differences in children's ability, personality, and social/emotional characteristics will depend somewhat on genetics (innate characteristics). At the same time, the environment does play an important role. The brain reorganizes itself, even into adulthood, as a result of stimuli from environmental factors and the learner's response to the stimuli (Bruer, 1998; Weiss, 2000).

Teachers and parents also grow in terms of their ability to provide appropriate environmental support. At age 1-1/2, Bruno was not talking at all, and his speech therapist often became frustrated. At one point the child refused to say "open" (a requirement to get his favorite toy), but instead would vigorously give a hand signal for "open." The therapist left, feeling a bit discouraged. Needing to return, however, she approached the garden gate where Bruno and his grandmother were playing. Bruno saw the therapist first and pointed energetically with his finger, saying loudly and clearly, "Open." He was duly rewarded and his oral language seemed to develop quite normally from that point. The grandmother then shared a story with the mother and therapist. Helena, Bruno's mother, also did not talk until age 1-1/2. She, too, was successful in pointing and gesturing to make herself understood. One day as she and her mother were walking the dog, the animal continually brought objects and dropped them in front of them and barked, "Woof, woof." Helena's mother would pat him, saying, "Good dog, good dog." Later, while the mother and Helena were playing quietly, the dog entered the room, and Helena shouted "Woof, woof." The mother exclaimed in great surprise, "Yes, he's a good dog." Helena then repeated, "Woof, woof, dud dod." Oral language had started to develop, and whole phrases emerged soon after.

Perhaps these incidents demonstrate that learning does not happen in a vacuum. Genetics could account for late development of oral language, but what role did the environment of frustration and concern play in the child's initial response? What role did a more relaxed atmosphere play in unleashing the child's interest in rewarding the adult with a verbal response? Although we may never understand the reasons, understanding the developmental differences in children, becoming familiar with their individual learning styles, and adjusting our responses to these differences and individualities can help us in teaching children, and ultimately extending their learning.

For the first two years of life, children learn through sensorimotor experiences that enable them to form beginning concepts about their immediate environment and develop language to relate to it. A young child feels, touches, and often tastes objects that are new to her. She may attempt to pick up a bean. In the process, she may squash it and get a piece of it on her fingers. Then, she may put the piece of bean in her mouth and say "bee, mmm," in imitation of her mother's description: "It's a bean and it's yummy." With children at this early age, parents and caregivers need to understand how a supportive environment encourages the interactive learning that is crucial to later development.

During the next six to seven years, from age 2 through approximately age 8, children are in the preoperational period of thinking. At this stage, children's thinking is characterized by an excessive reliance on perception instead of logic. Piaget's conservation experiments provided evidence of children's reliance on perception; for example, children in these studies could not recognize that the amount of a liquid or a solid did not change when moved to a differently shaped or sized container. It takes lots of experiences before children realize that there is the same amount of cereal in a high, narrow bowl as there is in a low, wide bowl. Over time, logic and experience inform the more sophisticated thinker that the amounts are the same; for the preoperational child, who is bound by her perceptions, however, the high, narrow bowl has more cereal (or the low, wide bowl does, depending on what she perceives as "bigger").

At the same time, children's ability to use symbols and imagery is growing, as reflected in the rapid growth of language. First using words for immediate things or actions and then using language for beginning steps in reasoning, children progress to learning increasingly abstract forms of oral and written language.

Nevertheless, whether children are 4, 5, 6, or 7 years old, their thinking is still bound to the real world; they do not yet have the intellectual freedom to make possible the contemplation of the hypothetical, to compare the ideal with the actual, or to be concerned about the discrepancies between this world and that which they imagine possible (Lefrancois, 2001). The young child, impatient to get to Gramma's, wishes the red light to change to green. When it does, he is convinced that his wishing caused the light to change. Reality for him is what he perceives to be happening.

After age 7 or 8, children are able to perform mental operations, although their thoughts are still bound to the real world. For example, children at this age can determine their classmates' height. They can comprehend that if Mary is taller than Bill and Bill is taller than Joe, then Mary must be taller than Joe. They can see the reality of the situation and thus reason logically. After 11 or 12 years of age, children will be able to think and reason abstractly. They can solve abstract problems such as: which is the farthest away, given that the library is farther than the fire station and the fire station is farther than the community hall? Such reasoning requires abstract thinking.

Because children's learning throughout the period of early childhood is governed by their preoperational thinking, whether at home, in preschool, or in kindergarten or primary classrooms, children learn through:

- Interactions as a result of their own social, mental, and physical activity
- Continuity of integrated experiences
- The use of language in conjunction with reflection.

INTERACTIONS

During the preoperational period of growth from age 2 to about 7 or 8, all children need to be mentally, socially, and physically active in order to learn. When activity centers are arranged throughout the preschool and primary rooms—with spaces for building, art, music, reading, board game play, dramatic play, writing, math, and science, plus time to use these spaces and materials—children have opportunities to learn through firsthand physical activity. Such activity centers have materials that provide for children's free exploration of a topic—for example, "Which

objects will sink and which ones will float? Can you make a sinking object float, or a floating object sink?" These centers also will include materials for learning specific skills, such as letter recognition, word study, or multiplication tables.

As children work in centers of interest, they are able to relate with one another. They comment on each other's work, spontaneously offering criticism and information as they exchange ideas and prior knowledge in a cooperative effort. The necessity to compromise, to adjust their thinking in response to the ideas of others, is real and invaluable for children's social, emotional, and intellectual growth. Vygotsky (1986) believed that this type of social activity was needed as the generator of thought: "The mechanism of social behavior and the mechanism of consciousness are the same" (Vygotsky, 1986, p. ii). One might say that relations with others builds individual consciousness. Helena's response to the dog is a dramatic illustration of this notion. This is also true when a child hit by another child acts startled. It is as if from this interaction, he suddenly realizes that hitting hurts.

CONTINUITY OF EXPERIENCES

Because children's growth is continuous from preschool through the primary grades, they require educational experiences that are equally continuous. Stated simply, this means that throughout the period of early childhood, one learning experience will build on another. A thread of meaning should run through a number of experiences. Hopefully, the experiences, activities, and lessons will be juxtaposed to enable children to see connections between the past and present, among and between people, and among the objects and events of their world.

An integrated curriculum or project approach provides curriculum in a way that emphasizes these connections. For example, in one multiage classroom, the unit for study was different modes of transportation. The teacher introduced the unit by having children bring photos of themselves going from one place to another. One child brought a picture showing her helping her grandfather drive a motorboat to an off-shore island; another child had a picture of him and his father in front of their plane, ready for a short hop to the coast. Others displayed photos of their families at the beginning of vacation trips. After showing their photos, as a class they classified them into land travel, water travel, and air travel. The pictures were compiled into a classroom mural, and the children wrote short stories about their special trips. The teacher and the children also read and shared books about various ways people travel.

With the children's questions in mind, the teacher arranged two trips: one to a nearby harbor and another to a railroad museum. Interest groups were formed around specific topics, and ability grouping allowed children to practice certain reading skills as they sought information. Children developed their geography and math skills as they found locations or figured out problems related to distance and travel. One group of children who became interested in different types of boats drew and constructed models. Vocabulary lists of new words, like "helicopter," "blimp," "speedboat," and "schooner," were compiled. As the lists grew longer, some children began to classify the words and others arranged the classified list alphabetically. The youngest children copied the listed words on special word cards and developed games to help them remember the words. In culminating experiences, each child produced a book of travel. Older children tended to write a story, while younger ones in the multiage room brought in pictures of transportation modes and wrote brief descriptions of each. Also, an experienced traveler came to class to describe his trip to Africa. He began his narrative by describing his car ride to the airport and the plane trip, and then included some of the walking trips he had taken in Africa. These types of experiences, according to Katz and Chard (2000), allow the chil-

dren to integrate skills and concepts into a continuous whole.

Continuity of experiences also means that curriculum from the preschool across the primary grades will be coordinated and continuous. As a group of primary school children goes to the harbor to observe the boats anchored there, the children will recall a previous trip during the preschool years and make links to the new trip and its purpose.

Experiences developed for skill building need continuity. Children cannot be asked to direct their own learning in the primary grades without a background of initiating their own learning during their preschool and kindergarten experiences. Children need time and opportunity to develop the skills involved in being self-directing, making plans, setting their own goals, and finding ways to achieve these goals. Before children in the 1st and 2nd grade will be able to write, they need opportunities to scribble and draw in preschool and kindergarten. They need to observe their own words written down and experiment with recording sounds as they hear them. These early literacy experiences prepare children, as they move into 1st and 2nd grade, to write a complete thought and even to compose a story.

COVERED WITH LANGUAGE

Children learn through activity centers because these centers make the need for language real and necessary. "Children not only speak about what they are doing, their speech and action are part of one and the same complex psychological function" (Vygotsky, 1986, p. iv). While talking, arguing, discussing, listening, reading, and writing, children clarify their experiences; at the same time, they are developing emotional and moral responses such as empathy, self-control, and assertiveness. Brain research indicates there are strong links between emotions and cognition (Jensen, 1998; Shonkoff & Phillips, 2000).

Children converse informally as they work

together on a puzzle, rotate eggs in an incubator, or construct a space station. They talk about what they are doing or tell about what happened yesterday or continue an argument that occurred on the playground. Allowing this type of talk in the classroom gives children the chance to practice their skills in explaining, clarifying, making points, and arguing over events, and it "contributes substantially to intellectual development in general, and literacy growth in particular" (Dyson, 1987, p. 397).

Teachers' language also is important as they intervene to model, question, and help children develop other ways of discussing or arguing. Tillie, a 1st-grader, became upset when her friend Mary said accusingly, "You told Aletha you didn't like me." "No, I didn't!" Tillie argued. "Uh huh, yes, you did!" Mary argued back. After a few moments of this dialogue, Tillie complained to the teacher. The teacher asked, "Did you ask what Aletha really said?" Tillie posed that question to Mary, who replied, "Aletha said you didn't like me when I copied your picture." "Well, I didn't," responded Tillie, "but I like you now that we're drawing our own pets." "Yeah, it's more fun," replied Mary, who now seemed pleased.

In addition to informal exchanges like these, the formal discussions that take place are equally important. Both large- and small-group discussions provide opportunities for children's growth and learning. When formal classroom discourse is the only mode of conversation, however, problems can emerge. Early research indicated that during typical discussions, teacher talk dominated, teachers selected the topics, and a dialogue pattern of teacher-question/child-response prevailed (Cook, Gumperz, & Gumperz, 1982; Flanders, 1970). Too often, this remains the pattern in many classrooms. If formal discussions are used exclusively, children have insufficient opportunities to initiate ideas, argue points, listen to other responses, or follow another's argument

(Cazden, 1986; Morine-Dershimer & Tenenberg, 1992). By thoughtfully planning large-group discussions, however, teachers can help children grow in their ability to follow an idea, argue a point, and listen to others' viewpoints. Following up through small-group discussions can provide the practice for appropriate group interactions. These follow-up sessions should be both planned and spontaneous. The spontaneous sessions often provide teachers with valuable insights into children's achievements.

REFLECTION

Learning requires reflection. Throughout the preschool and primary grades, children need to be able to think about what they have done, and to reflect on their actions and ideas if they are to learn. They should be encouraged to: 1) organize their ideas and experiences, 2) communicate and present their findings to others, 3) apply what they have learned, and 4) evaluate their work.

1. Organizing Their Ideas and Experiences. Children can organize their ideas by drawing a picture, writing a story, making a graph or chart, constructing a bulletin, or creating a display. As children engage in these experiences, the skilled teacher observes and, when appropriate, offers suggestions to help children organize their experiences. If a child dashes off one creation and "is done," the teacher might engage him in recalling events that led to his drawing this particular picture. Children writing stories are often able to extend the stories if the teacher helps them recall the sequence of events. Before making individual graphs or charts, children need to participate in making group graphs or charts of classroom events. In one classroom, a teacher used stickers of different fruits. As children selected the fruit they liked best, they placed their stickers in the appropriate column on the prepared graph paper. Children could then tell which fruit was most popular. By laminating the graph, the class could study students' many different preferences, and at the same time develop their graphing skills.

In one 1st-grade classroom, the children charted the monthly weather by placing a picture representing the particular weather on a homemade calendar. At the end of the month, the children could determine the number of rainy days, sunny days, cloudy days, etc. during the month. They also could determine which week had the best weather overall for that month.

2. Communicating and Presenting Their Findings to Others. Even 4- and 5-year-olds can be asked to communicate their ideas and work to others. Rather than always asking preschool children to share during the morning opening group time, it is useful to invite sharing *after* the children's work time. Then, children can tell the group how they made something or what they accomplished during work time. This gives them the opportunity not only to organize their ideas and experiences, but also to communicate and present these to others. While some children seem to grow into this ability naturally, others need to have the skill nurtured. One kindergarten teacher who regularly used this technique found that by the end of the day one of her 5-year-olds always forgot what he wanted to share. She began to remind him during work time that he would be asked to share what he was doing. Then, she would briefly rehearse his presentation with him in private. Initially, she would ask him to tell what he did first to make his object and what his next step was. As he became able to describe his actions during the class discussion without prompting, she then asked him to relate more elaborate steps. Gradually, he became skilled at sharing without her assistance.

3. Applying What They Have Learned. As new projects or topics are begun, both teacher and children reflect on what they have learned and how they can apply the new knowledge or skill to a new task. As they learned about land masses, a 3rd-grade class acquired the skill of segmenting words into parts, which they needed to figure out the word *peninsula*. After they learned how to segment one word, the children began to use that skill to read other unknown words. In addition, the children, who previously had learned how to measure the area of their sand table, applied and transformed those measuring skills to the task of figuring out how much material they needed to cover the floor of their playhouse.

4. Evaluating Their Work. Children should be asked to think about and evaluate their own progress and work in both informal and formal ways. Even 4- and 5-year-olds can be asked to make judgments about what they did and learned during the day. After several trials, one 5-year-old in the block area figured out how to balance a particular block for his construction. An astute teacher observed his efforts and asked him to share with the class how he had accomplished the task. Although he needed the blocks—the concrete materials—as props to accompany his evaluation of his accomplishment, he was able to tell the other children that it took "patience, and I had to keep trying." Children in the primary grades can keep records of their stories and checklists of the skills they've learned, and thus can compare their current work to that completed at the beginning of the school year. Many teachers use portfolios of children's work as a means of assessment; the children can help choose appropriate items for inclusion in their portfolios. Gradually, children learn to explain why their choice is important and how a chosen piece of work demonstrates their progress. By doing so, children monitor their own learning, set their own goals, and experience the joy and satisfaction of accomplishing these goals.

THE PROBLEM

It is no secret; today's schools are under great pressure. Children's success often has been interpreted to mean achieving a predetermined standard within a given grade. To reach this goal, many school districts have adopted rigid schedules and curricula, establishing specific content for different grade levels. This highly prescribed curriculum is considered a way for all children to achieve local and national objectives, performance standards, and competencies within a given time frame.

When inflexible policies exist, however, education is treated like a timed test. Only those children who master age-grade content are permitted to enter school or move on to the next grade. Children are judged inadequate or unready for placement in the next group if they have not mastered the content.

Scores on standardized achievement tests become the yardstick of success. Because they are thought to document success, test scores became more important than ensuring children's development. Curriculum is often designed around the content of the test, not around the children's past experiences, needs, interests, or developmental levels. As a result of such standardization, children's early experiences in many schools have become structured and teacher-centered. Children's play and creative activities are limited (Lubeck, 2000). Many kindergarten and primary classes have come to look or sound like any other classroom in the "all eyes on me" teacher-directed school, where all children wait (often rowdily) for teacher cues in order to focus. Instead of children learning by interacting with others and by observing and experimenting with how things work, they are expected to learn by sitting still, listening, and following instructions.

Young children who are still in the preoperational stage of thinking will have difficulty learning when the curriculum is designed to teach them a set of abstract and isolated academic skills within a given time frame. Unable to make sense of isolated and abstract content, and denied the opportunity to learn through their own physical, mental, and social-emotional activities, children often fail. In fact, in the many areas of the United States where the only acceptable method of measuring success is using standardized tests, schools are finding that children do not perform well. The curriculum often becomes test-driven, even in early childhood classrooms, and the focus is given mainly to phonics and reading. When one subject takes precedence to the exclusion of other content, however, the integration of important skills often suffers, and these children then may do poorly in math and writing.

Yet teachers who do have the ability to adapt their classrooms, so that all children become active learners, discover that their students' test scores do not suffer. One teacher, at the end of the school year, discovered that her "less than average" class had the highest scores for 3rd-graders in the school. She attributed their success to changes she had made as a result of reorganizing her Morning Meeting time, whereby the children learned to respect one another, help each other, assume responsibility, maintain self-control, and assert themselves in positive ways (Bondy & Ketts, 2002). The teacher believed that these skills transferred to other areas of the classroom; for example, instead of fooling around, the children became more task-oriented when helping and supporting each other.

The way many schools operate today brings to mind the Greek myth of Procrustes, referred to by Goodlad and Anderson (1959) in their classic text, *The Nongraded Elementary School*. When travelers sought Procrustes's house for shelter, he tied them to an iron bedstead. If the traveler were shorter than the bed, Procrustes stretched the person to the same length as the bed. If the person were longer, limbs were chopped off so the person could fit the bed. Procrustes shaped both short and tall until they were equally long and dead.

Developmental continuity is jeopardized when schools use Procrustean methods to force children into fitting the system, instead of adapting the system to fit the child. Children entering kindergarten with a background of learning in child-centered, play-oriented programs find the early academic demands of many kindergartens confusing, stressful, and sometimes impossible to achieve. In response, schools have implemented a number of policies. Some screen children on a variety of measures, and systematically exclude from educational programs those deemed "unready." Others have raised the entrance age so that only older children—those who have a better chance, developmentally, of achieving the fixed curriculum—will be in school. In both cases, the child is required to be "ready" to fit the school. Who are these schools for, and whose interests are being served by such policies?

Ultimately, inflexible organizational policies have a "trickle down" effect on the child care, nursery, and preschool communities. Desperate to prepare children for kindergarten and the primary grades, many preschools are becoming more academic in nature. Thinking that earlier introduction to isolated academic skills will better prepare children for the rigors of the accelerated academic kindergarten and primary grades, many preschools limit children's active learning in favor of stressing the alphabet, spelling words, and number facts in a prescribed, sequential, and isolated fashion. They have foregone or misinterpreted the value of constructive play—a chance to experiment and interact with educational toys and natural materials, and with their peers and significant adults.

Even when children's preschool experiences correspond to their developmental progress, problems can still emerge later in public school. Children accustomed to learning through play and activity, and encouraged to make decisions and gain autonomy, find the adjustment to academic kindergarten to be difficult. The continuity of learning so necessary throughout the early years is disrupted as children move from the preschool to the very different educational experience to be found in the elementary school. Intellectual curiosity, excitement about learning, important thinking skills, and knowledge about one's world can be sadly thwarted by rigid curricula that require children to learn isolated skills and facts.

Given this situation, there is a sense of urgency to promote developmental continuity across the preschool and primary years. We believe that if the curriculum continually responds to children's learning patterns—to individual, cultural, and linguistic diversity—then so many children will not fail. Larger numbers of children will find school to be a place where they can achieve, find respect, and continue to grow emotionally as well as intellectually—not a place where children become failures if they do not measure up to the "norm." In our constant efforts to improve test scores, rarely have we given teachers opportunities to improve their abilities in determining children's level of development, their prior learning, or their cultural differences. Nor have we been willing to provide the time or resources to enable teachers, administrators, parents, and community members to work together effectively.

CONTINUITY ACROSS THE YEARS

Concern for developmental continuity across the preschool and primary grades is not new. It may well have started with the establishment of the first kindergarten programs in the United States in the late 1880s. The first kindergartens, probably much like today's child care centers or preschools, were operated by philanthropic individuals, churches, and other civic and charitable organizations.

A great deal of emphasis on social services and family support was evident in these early programs. The *kindergartners*, as the teachers were called, "prided themselves on their ability to establish relationships with families and to perform socially beneficial tasks" (Beatty, 1989, p. 77). The curriculum in these first kindergartens, which revolved around Froebel's gifts and occupations, was one of play and activity.

Because of their popularity, the first kindergartens soon became a part of the public school system. Once programs for 5-year-olds were housed in public schools, however, changes occurred. The kindergarten teachers found little time for home visits or community work and, instead of being able to follow the traditional Froebelian curriculum of play, they were pressured to get the children ready for 1st grade.

Conflict ensued. The kindergarten teachers who wanted to "bring more enjoyment and more socializing experiences into children's lives" (Parker & Temple, 1925, p. 2) resisted integration with primary grades. On the other hand, primary teachers found fault with the "kindergartners" (kindergarten teachers). They believed "kindergartners failed to recognize the importance of the essential social skills in reading, writing, and arithmetic, which the primary school historically has emphasized in response to defined social needs" (p. 2).

Attempting to establish more continuity between the kindergarten and 1st grade, Samuel Parker and Alice Temple published *Unified Kindergarten and First-Grade Teaching* in 1925. They stressed that because children's mental abilities were the same from kindergarten through 1st grade, there should be no break in methods and kindergarten and 1st-grade curricula should be "continuous and delightful" (Parker & Temple, 1925, p. 1).

Parker and Temple (1925) advocated that play activities, social interactions, and units of science and nature continue through the 1st grade, and that kindergarten children be introduced to skill development, reading readiness activities, and science and math content. Their notions are still very current.

NONGRADED UNITS

Efforts to make children's education continuous throughout the early years did not end with Parker and Temple. During the 1940s and early 1950s, nongraded primary units

were created to address children's different capacities. These nongraded primary units were not conceived as a method of teaching, "nor [as] a departure from established procedures long used by good teachers, but rather as an administrative tool to encourage and promote a philosophy of continuous growth" (Milwaukee Public Schools [MPS], 1942, p. 3). Instead of making the child fit into the administrative system of the schools, through nongraded units the administrative system could fit the nature of the child. Each child progressed at her or his own level in these primary units. Progress, whether fast or slow, was observed and recorded, and teaching was adjusted to the needs of each individual child. A number of basal reading series and mathematics, science, and social studies texts were available in each school. These were categorized by level and shared among teachers. With this abundance of materials, every child's level of maturation theoretically could be matched to appropriate materials. Educators believed this individualized instruction and unity of program, from the kindergarten through grade 3, would eliminate the "piling up of problems at the end of the primary school period" (MPS, 1942, p. 4).

The units, however, had problems. Evaluation was weak. Teachers alone were given the complex task of judging each child's progress and achievement. With no standardized form, reporting a child's progress was problematic, and parents often misunderstood the intent of the program. They were often very vocal about their need to know exactly what grade their children were in and to which grade they would be promoted in the following year. In truth, well-developed nongraded kindergarten and primary units were the exception at this time, not the rule.

Nor did these units last very long. In 1957, the Soviets launched the first human-made satellite—Sputnik—into outer space, and the space race was on. Public pressure for achievement, especially in math and science, that would put American children ahead of those in Russia, Germany, or any other nation, was intense.

Educators responded with equal intensity. Many, in order to document children's achievement, focused the curriculum on isolated academic skills in order show children's achievement within a given time frame. Content appropriate for children in the 4th or 5th grade was moved down to the 2nd or 3rd grade, so that children would have to work harder and become more able to take their place among the successful scientists of the world. In this intense atmosphere, the peaceful, kind, and fair nongraded units of the 1940s and 1950s, with a few isolated exceptions, disappeared.

CONCERN, CONTINUED

Concern for developmental continuity did not disappear along with the demise of nongraded units, however. In the late 1960s, concern for continuity between preschool and elementary school led to development of new programs. Research indicating that Head Start children's achievement gains dissipated by the end of kindergarten or the 1st grade promoted the then federal Office of Education to fund Project Follow Through, implementation of which would provide greater continuity of curriculum from Head Start through grade 3. Follow Through projects followed a specific curriculum model. Communities selected one of several models and implemented it across Head Start and the elementary grades.

Similar concerns led to the funding of Project Developmental Continuity (PDC) by the U.S. Department of Education in 1974. A national Head Start demonstration program, PDC was designed to promote continuity of curriculum and comprehensive child development services for children as they made the transition from Head Start to school. The project was based on the assumption that children's continuous and gradual growth and learning are enhanced when educational programs are planned according to each child's needs, and flow out of previous experiences in the home and school.

As it turned out, however, neither Project Follow Through nor Project Developmental Continuity was found to be completely effective in promoting continuity of children's early educational experiences. Each was found to be related to positive gains for some children, but neither entirely fulfilled its stated purposes (Kagan & Neuman, 1997; Seefeldt & Barbour, 1998). It appears impossible to design a curriculum model that can be implemented with equally successful results for all children in a community. Effective curriculum cannot be imposed on children. It takes the concerted effort of the entire community to develop educational systems that are congruent with children's experiences in their home, school, and community (Barbour & Barbour, 2001).

Over the years, curriculum innovators have continued to design programs with the intent of making children's education responsive to their developmental levels. At the same time, differing political climates put pressure on schools to focus on specific skill development to meet the challenges of rapidly changing technological advances and world globalization.

Multiage grouping, nongraded instructional groups, family grouping, and multiage continuous programs, although few in number across the United States, continue to be implemented with varying degrees of success. Despite varying strategies and techniques, these approaches all have similar underlying philosophies and similar requirements for success. The nongraded or multiage types of instruction, with an adjustable curriculum, mean that children enter a unit at a specific age and stay in that unit for at least two or three years. "Family style classrooms" are very similar arrangements (Gaustad, 1998).

Looping, often referred to as "teacher rotation," is a similar idea in that it enhances a child's continual growth. It was tried as early as 1913—again, with varying amounts of success. In looping, instead of including different ages in one classroom, the teacher moves from one grade level to the next with the children. This strategy gives teachers more time to analyze children's individual growth patterns, try out a variety of teaching techniques, and establish better relationships with families and community. Gaustad (1998) has suggested that such grouping is easier for teachers to accomplish before moving into a multiage grouping plan. In looping, teachers grow and experience new curriculum along with the children, rather than facing the sudden need to revamp the entire curriculum to fit different ages in a multiage arrangement.

Curriculum designers and innovators recommend a wide variety of strategies to support learning for all children. Integrated curriculum, the project approach, cooperative learning, and balanced literacy programs are a few methods that feature a developmental focus, offering specific strategies and techniques for enriched curricula. All these programs have had some measure of success.

Research indicates that students achieve greater success when the program (no matter what kind) has the following characteristics:

- A belief that children have different learning rates and styles
- A view that individualized teaching and developmental continuity are achievable
- A commitment to regarding children's learning as being on a continuum of development, rather than based on predetermined age or grade designations
- An understanding of the stages of child development, as well as the variations in that development
- An understanding of appropriate curriculum and content and the skills needed to master this content
- A large repertoire of instructional strategies and a wide range of evaluation procedures
- Successful collaboration among teachers, parents, and community members
- A recognition that the entire school community affects the learning process
- A realization that successful teachers learn to work cooperatively with all aspects of the school community to achieve good programs for children.

As teachers strive to introduce developmental continuity in their classrooms, they can choose from an array of ideas. If new ideas are to succeed, teachers must be involved in the planning of any innovation. To truly implement good teaching, however, teachers need to carefully select what will work for them in their classrooms at any given time. Large class sizes, the growing complexity of society, and the overwhelming problems some children bring into the schools put great stresses on the classroom teacher. Yet, the situation demands attention more than ever. Communities must provide the resources for schools to succeed in educating every child according to his/her ability.

CHAPTER 2

TOWARD DEVELOPMENTAL CONTINUITY: GETTING STARTED

"How did it all get started in your school system?" Claudia asks in another session. "Well," answers Consuela, "it is difficult to tell where it all started, but I think that a kindergarten teacher and a 1st-grade teacher approached their principal to suggest redesigning their classrooms so that children in their rooms could have a more continuous flow of instruction. Both teachers had several parents who worked in their classrooms, so they enlisted these parents in the planning process. What exists now is the result of evolution that continues as we learn more about our successes and failures."

Turning to Laverne, Consuela continues, "The National Head Start Program has long been concerned with easing the transition of Head Start children into the public school system and has many recommendations to make. However, the actual task of doing so still hasn't been achieved. It takes the concerted effort of teachers and administrators to accomplish real continuity of learning. Your task may be easier since your program is already in an elementary school."

Providing children with a continuum of educational experiences that respond to their development across the preschool and primary grades can begin with a single teacher (or a group of teachers) and a single classroom or unit. Actually, anyone, or any one group, can make the decision to work to provide continuity in children's learning, in school programs, and in the classroom curriculum. Change can begin at the grassroots level, with one or two teachers, a principal, or a group of parents taking leadership (Wells, 1994). Or change might be initiated at the administrative level by the school board, superintendent, or other school supervisor. Regardless of who initiates the project (Miller & Kantrov, 1997), the support and cooperation of the larger community, parents, preschool and child care teachers, plus the business community, will be necessary.

Change will take different evolutionary forms, depending on the nature of the program, the school community, and other people involved. Projects and programs can be informal, even spontaneous, or they can be structured and systematized. Some programs are simple; others are highly complex.

A project can be as easy, yet as useful, as creating a paper form to record children's progress from preschool through the primary grades. Or, it can be as informal as a group of 1st- and 2nd-grade teachers within a school deciding to work together to create a curriculum that continues from one grade to the next. Simple projects and programs can lead to such major system-wide changes as restructuring kindergarten/primary units or replacing standardized testing with developmentally appropriate assessment methods.

PROJECTS AIMED AT CONTINUITY

The following programs illustrate ways to provide developmental continuity. Some are simple ideas, easily implemented; others are more complex. These projects range from nationally organized ones to state and regional projects to locally implemented ideas.

NATIONAL PROJECTS

• The Northwest Regional Educational Laboratory, through its School Improvement Research Series (SIRS) Research You Can Use (NWREL, 2001), examines the research on the nature and effectiveness of primary schools, the rationale for implementing a nongraded primary unit, and recommendations from the research on how to implement a primary unit.
• The National Center for Early Development and Learning, Kindergarten Transition Project (Kraft-Sayre & Pianta, 2000) describes an approach to enhancing children's transitions to kindergarten. It focuses on building a network of social connections that support children, their families, and teachers as children make the transition from preschool to kindergarten.

• To enable Head Start children to maintain gains through the primary grades, the Administration of Children, Youth, and Families has initiated the Head Start-Public School Transition Demonstration project (1999). The project's purpose is to develop successful strategies whereby Head Start programs, parents, and local education agencies and other community agencies can cooperate in planning and implementing a continuous program of comprehensive services beginning in Head Start and continuing through kindergarten and the first three grades of public school.

• *Eager To Learn: Educating Our Preschoolers* (National Research Council, 2001) focuses on the effectiveness of early educational programs on children's development and learning. Although not directly pertaining to Head Start children's transition to school, it does offer a comprehensive overview of the complex conditions that foster children's growth and development. Ideas from this project can help teams developing continuity programs by providing some understanding of what can promote smooth transitions.

• The Administration for Children, Youth, and Families of the Department of Health and Human Services developed a multimedia kit, *Easing the Transition: From Preschool to Kindergarten. A Guide for Early Childhood Teachers and Administrators* (1988), based on Bronfenbrenner's (1979) thesis that transitions from one setting to another can be structured to enhance human potential. This program offers parents, teachers, and administrators suggestions for promoting continuity from children's preschool experiences to that of the kindergarten.

STATE AND REGIONAL PROJECTS

• The State of Missouri has developed *Project Construct* (1991), which implements Piagetian-based curriculum in preschools, kindergartens, and the primary grades. Teacher training, materials, and support for schools changing from teacher-centered curriculum to Piagetian-based curriculum are provided.

• In an attempt to promote continuity across the children's preschool and primary school experiences, the St. Louis Association for the Education of Young Children and the Southwestern Association for the Education of Young Children developed an *Early Childhood Transfer Form* (1989) to provide information about individuals and their prior experiences.

• The State of New Jersey's education department developed a *Guide for Teachers, Administrators, Parents, and Parent Coordinators: Planning for Parental Involvement in Early Childhood Education* (1989). The guide suggests many ways parents can work with schools and become involved in promoting education that responds to children's developmental level.

• The *Maryland Model for School Readiness* (Maryland State Department of Education, 1998) was developed in response to National Education Goal 1, which calls for all children to start school ready to learn. In addition to establishing a systematic assessment method using the Work Sampling System (Rebus, Inc., 2001) or a compatible assessment for all prekindergarten, kindergarten, and preschool special education programs in the public schools, the model aims to enhance communication among teachers, early care providers, and families about children's specific strengths and needs as they make the transition from early care and education to primary level education.

• The State of Kentucky's school reform initiatives that began in the early 1990s included a mandate to develop nongraded primary units in all public schools from kindergarten through the 3rd grade. A discussion of the implementation of the primary units, problems that arose, and success stories can be found in the Implementation of Educational Policy Analysis Archives (http://epaa.asu.edu). Ellen McIntyre and Diane Kyle's *Nongraded Primary Programs: Possibilities for Improving Practice for Teachers* (2002) offers an account of how teachers implemented nongraded primary units.

• Oregon's State House Bill 3565 (2001) includes provisions for review of nongraded models and a feasibility study of statewide implementation of nongraded primary units.

LOCAL PROJECTS

• In Washington, D.C., the Office of Early Education in the District of Columbia Public schools joined forces with the National Day Care Association, a Head Start grantee, and Teaching Strategies, Inc., a private materials development and training firm, in a three-year effort to promote continuity of children's early educational experiences. Strategies to ease children's transition from Head Start to the public schools were implemented, and training for teachers and parents in developmentally appropriate curriculum across the preschool and primary grades was conducted.

• In Anne Arundel County, Maryland, the Superintendent's Task Force on Early Childhood Education was formed in 1997 and charged with, among other tasks, exploring and creating connections among community resources that support the achievement and social growth of young children from diverse backgrounds. Since that time, public school teachers have presented information about school readiness at a yearly child care conference and are continuing to implement the recommendations of the task force (http://aacps.org) in regard to supporting young children's academic achievement through collaboration among schools, community groups, and families.

• A principal of a Boston school created a mini-nongraded unit. Time was given for kindergarten, 1st-, and 2nd-grade teachers to meet and plan the program together. Materials were collected that could be used by all children in any group. Reporting procedures were changed to respond to children's continuing progress.

• In another school, kindergarten and 1st-grade teachers met and agreed to adapt their instruction to children's maturational levels, instead of the published curriculum. This school's changes began with just one kindergarten and one 1st-grade teacher, who met during the summer to plan a curriculum that would begin in kindergarten and continue through 1st grade. Throughout the year, the two teachers discussed the progress of the children, individually and as a group. At the end of the school year, the kindergarten teacher reviewed the progress of each child and the experiences of the total group. Based on this information, the two teachers made plans for the beginning of 1st grade. These teachers' success encouraged other teachers in the school to organize team meetings; by the third year, all teachers at every grade level were planning together to meet children's developmental levels.

PRINCIPLES OF PLANNING

Developing continuity programs can begin with a simple plan or a complex one. Success depends on committed people who are willing to find out about other successful programs, define what they are attempting to do, become skilled in communicating their ideas to others, accept others' involvement, receive authorization for implementing their plans, and, after achieving an initial success, make plans for expanding the program. During the many phases of implementation, parents and the community need to be aware of the steps being taken and the progress of the children. Any committed person can initiate the process; without the involvement of other committed individuals, however, only minimal success is possible.

COMMITMENT

Regardless of the program type, whether there are changes in classroom practice, curriculum, or school structure, commitment is key. Without commitment based on knowledge and understanding, the best-laid plans and truest intentions will fail. Open-space classrooms, built in such abundance during the 1970s, were intended to provide curriculum that would match children's needs for active learning with others. However, far too many classrooms were designed with the expectation that teachers, principals, and parents would automatically understand the concept and initiate change. Although there were many successes, many teachers found the open space design disconcerting. Therefore, teachers often use partitions to define smaller spaces within the classroom.

The teacher who wants to begin changing the curriculum and school will need to find someone with whom to work. While a single teacher can change programs and curriculum within a school system, a group of teachers working together is more likely to achieve success (Wells, 1994). Working with someone else provides a support system and supplies feedback on one's ideas—both successes and failures.

Teachers who seek change generally benefit from partnerships with colleagues, but they also need to recognize that change is a gradual, evolutionary process, not a revolutionary one. Teachers in the British Infant Schools were successful because they recognized this truth. When asked how she managed to create programs that continually responded to children's development, one U.K. teacher replied:

"You Americans! You're always so eager for a revolution, when what you need is evolution. We didn't just change from a rigid, authoritarian program overnight—we evolved our programs. It took time for us to evolve our philosophy, our ideas, and even more time for parents and others to evolve. But taking time was necessary for our

Head Mistresses and Masters, the parents, and our entire system to unite in their commitment to making changes that would last."

Finding Out

How can you find out more about developmental continuity across the preschool and primary grades? Teachers might begin by reading everything they can about developmental continuity and finding someone with whom to discuss the ideas. An examination of the research and theory of developmental continuity and programs not only will increase one's understanding of continuity, but also provide insights into how to design, plan, and implement one's own program.

Next, teachers could visit and observe a number of ongoing successful programs. Although these visits serve a number of purposes, the visits are often most beneficial in terms of psychological support. Nongraded programs, or any other program of developmental continuity, look so normal in practice that many educators feel reassured and confident about changing their current practice or programs. Chase and Doan (1994), for example, offer a detailed look at their own multiage classroom as well as the experiences of a diverse group of practitioners across the United States.

Defining

In reading about and observing programs, teachers will discover diverse ways of changing practices within their schools and communities. Examples of what they can use include the following:

- When communicating with parents about their children's growth, prekindergarten teachers in Calvert County, Maryland, decided to use narrative descriptions in place of the standard report card.
- A Branch of the Association of Childhood Education International created a reporting form about their individual preschool experiences that children could take with

them to elementary school.
- A group of 1st-grade teachers participated in a workshop on art as a means of early symbolization. They discovered that some children who were having difficulty with the structured reading and writing program were able to express their ideas and feelings by painting.
- A school board designed and implemented a multiage program that spanned kindergarten through 2nd grade.
- In another community, child care teachers arranged for their children to visit the "big" school before their entrance into kindergarten.
- First-, 2nd-, and 3rd-grade teachers in four schools constituting a region of a large school system developed a regional program of developmental continuity. Their program included uniform methods of reporting children's progress and a continuum of experiences and projects suited to the community's culture and resources.
- One group of 2nd-grade teachers who wanted to change their approach to spelling activities informed parents and their principal that they were going to encourage children's writing by experimenting with spelling, discovering patterns, formulating spelling rules, and uncovering exceptions to the rules.

With so many diverse directions to travel, a teacher or administrator with previous experience in challenging the system can help to develop clear procedures for beginning the process. Here is one teacher's action plan:

- State your purpose for change in a clear and straightforward manner.
- Specify the goals and objectives necessary to achieve the purpose.
- Decide on the scope and breadth of the program.
- Determine the requisite procedures for fulfilling the objectives.
- Enlist involvement of others.

- Locate resources within the school and in the school system.
- Decide how to evaluate the success of the innovations.

With Consuela's encouragement, Claudia and Laverne began to change the curriculum in their classrooms. They were a ready-made team working in the same school. They decided to try out specific curriculum practices in their classrooms that would cohere with the work in the other. They began by initiating a number of strategies suggested by the project approach (Helm & Katz, 2001) and balanced literacy practices (Schickedanz, 1999). They determined what parts of their program and practices they would change and how they would evaluate their success.

Over the next six months they tried out different ideas, meeting to share their successes and fret over the things they tried that turned out less than wonderfully. They revised plans and made additional changes, supporting one another.

COMMUNICATING

Dewey (1944) believed that unless one could effectively communicate ideas to others, clarity of thought was impossible. Likewise, Claudia and Laverne believed that it was important to practice their communication skills with each other. They took turns describing their program and intentions to each other, detailing:

- The purpose, goals, and intent of their proposed changes
- Some of the possible benefits to children, the school system, parents, and teachers
- The theory and research supporting their program
- Possible costs and benefits that would accrue.

Confident of their ability to articulate their plans clearly and think on their feet, Claudia and Laverne began the process of involving others.

INVOLVING OTHERS

Many teachers have attempted to make changes within their classrooms, only to discover great resistance from parents who do not support or understand the modifications. By involving others, teachers have found other voices that support the changes and can articulate to others the value of these changes for children.

Paul's mother and Valerie's father were regular volunteers in Claudia's classroom. Active in the PTA, they were excited about working to support their children's teachers. Claudia had organized a class trip to the harbor so the children could watch a ship dock. She was thrilled with the stories the children had dictated afterwards, and explained to the parents,

"In the past, I always had the children fill out workbook pages to identify beginning sounds related to pictures. This year, Laverne and I decided to see if another strategy, better suited to children's maturation, would work. Because we wanted children to initiate some of their own learning activities, we followed their interest in boats and transportation with a trip to the harbor.

"At the harbor, the children became interested in different types of boats as well as the names on the boats. We then took photos of the children in front of 'their boat,' and then we each made a collage of all the pictures for our classroom. My children used this collage to copy the names of the boats into their journals. I found that by asking the children the initial sound in their boat names, they became intrigued and began to group the boats according to the similar sounds they heard. This strategy got children interested in grouping other things according to initial sounds, like their names, their favorite foods, and their pets. Laverne got her children interested in letter names in a similar fashion.

"We both began to move away from workbooks; at first, we used the skills to be developed from the workbooks. As we related children's learning to their experiences, we found children practicing their skills in their informal class time. We shared this experience first with Paul's and Valerie's parents, who carried out the practice at home."

Daily, Claudia and Laverne met with their parent volunteers to describe and explain the changes they were making. The possibilities of changing the curriculum to be more responsive to young children's development intrigued the parents. Excited by the changes they were observing in the classroom, they, in turn, talked with other parents.

Claudia first approached those parents already volunteering in her classroom. Communication with parents can be done through conferences, home visits, informal notes, telephone calls, or parent bulletin boards. If these traditional modes of communicating are ineffective, new approaches might work. For example, inviting parents to an evening meeting where the teacher demonstrates new approaches and parents actually participate in the program in the same way as their child would can be very effective. Through hands-on experiences in centers, parents can begin to appreciate the value of active learning. Involving parent volunteers in this way can add another dimension to the program, as these parents can offer firsthand accounts of the children's eager participation in the new approach. Collecting samples of children's work to demonstrate their progress can be a particularly effective way of convincing parents of the program's value.

Both Claudia and Laverne found they had a group of parents who were willing to bring in resources, work with individual children, and suggest other experiences for the class. With the principal's support, this group of parents began to contact other parents, helping them to understand how the classroom changes were providing more continuity of experiences for their children.

RECEIVING AUTHORIZATION

Feeling validated by the parents' support and enthusiastic responses, Claudia and Laverne held further meetings with their principal.

Buttressed with samples of the children's work, a written statement of their goals and intentions, and reprints of several articles about developmentally appropriate curriculum, they described the changes they had made over the past months. They asked for authorization to continue developing methods of responding to children's developmental needs.

Although many changes are and can be made in the classroom without authorization, significant changes will require some type of authorization. Local and state policies need to be examined and studied. The flexibility of these policies, and any parameters that cannot be changed, must be identified. Many changes can be made that fit within the parameters of stated policies, while other plans may first require changes in policies.

Different school systems will require authorization from different sources. In Milwaukee, Wisconsin, during the beginning days of moving from separate primary grades to a nongraded primary unit, teachers in one school began to eliminate age-grade placement by changing the name plates outside their rooms. They removed the signs saying *Grade 1, 2,* and so on and replaced them with *Ms. Smith, NON-GRADED PRIMARY UNIT*. Before they did so, however, they asked their principal for authorization. By getting his approval first, the teachers had strong support in their corner when parents and state supervisors asked about the change.

A kindergarten teacher in another school district decided she did not like measuring her children's progress by checking off competencies achieved. She asked her principal if they could both meet with the school board to discuss an alternative. Describing and illustrating how she had reported children's progress to parents by using narrative systems of anecdotal records, she asked permission to discard the competency list of separated and isolated skills and instead continue using her narratives. This teacher's strategy of partnering with her principal before meeting with the school board gave her the necessary support to make her case for change.

Teachers in another school district received authorization from the school board to experiment with a narrative system. They became so bogged down with writing elaborate narratives, however, that they requested permission to devise their own developmental lists. As they experimented, they enlisted parental support and feedback. In the end, they developed a form that most teachers, parents, and administrators found to be truly representative of the children's growth. The teachers in this district discovered that by seeking permission to experiment and make changes, they established better communications with the school board and the community.

Convinced by Claudia and Laverne's ability to articulate their ideas and by the documentation of children's success and their enthusiasm for learning, their principal agreed to work toward structuring developmental continuity across the school's kindergarten and primary grades. Other teachers were invited to meet with Claudia and Laverne; eventually, a Head Start/kindergarten/primary team was formed.

EXPANDING

Beginning small seems to guarantee a measure of success. When working with a few teachers or small groups of children, it is easier to control more variables, change methods that do not work, refine and polish methods that have potential, build the comfort level of all involved, and perfect practices. If the goal is to provide continuity of children's educational experiences across the preschool and primary grades, however, then expansion and the involvement of many more individuals and groups will be necessary as the ideas take hold.

Expansion of developmental continuity to the upper grades often occurs with successful nongraded primary units or when multiage groupings are present within a school. Other teachers notice the intense involvement of neighboring children in their own learning, and their enhanced achievement. Impressed with this achievement, teachers in the upper grades can be involved in continuing to respond to children's developmental needs throughout the elementary school grades.

Even beyond the primary grades, children will continue to respond best to teachers who engage them in active learning, who support their intellectual curiosity and pursuits, and who build on their accomplishments from their primary years. Miletta (1996) discusses appropriate curriculum practices in the elementary grades that support children who have been involved in preschool/primary programs of developmental continuity. If developmental continuity is to succeed, then others within the school system and throughout the larger community must be involved and committed to creating a continuous program throughout the preschool/primary and elementary grades that is responsive to children's developmental levels.

INVOLVING PARENTS

At the very least, parents will need to be informed of changes within a given school. A continuum of communication techniques can be used to inform parents and gain their commitment. These techniques include:

• *Notes explaining any new process or change in the curriculum.* One 1st-grade teacher anticipated that parents would be upset when they saw spelling errors in their children's stories, so she sent home an explanatory letter. She began, "Dear Parent, you may note misspelled words in your children's written work. This is because we are asking children to form a habit of writing without worrying about correct form at first. Thus, they are encouraged to write the word as they hear it." She continued to explain the rationale for proceeding in this manner as children

learn to read and write, and also noted that correct spelling would be a part of the children's learning about revising, editing, and publishing their written work.

• *An open-door policy for parent observations, with continued invitations to visit in the classroom and to volunteer.* One 2nd-grade teacher found that the children in his classroom were not able to do as many projects as he and they wanted because of a lack of parent volunteers. After discussing this dilemma together, teachers and students decided to embark on a campaign to get full parent involvement. They started by making a list of all the things a parent could do to support the classroom activities. Then, they outlined some of their planned projects and brainstormed some of the ways they thought parents might help. Some suggestions were traditional (e.g., providing materials, helping in the classroom, and baking cookies). Others were more original. One child mentioned that his father might be able to videotape their play, while another indicated that his father could help them identify the rocks they found in the park. The teacher then sent a letter home informing parents of the class's campaign and some of the suggestions, asking for their input. As the parents replied, the teacher devised a schedule and kept parents informed, through notes, verbal communication, and the class "newspaper," of the various projects and types of support that was needed.

• *Making certain products that are sent home illustrate children's learning, work, and progress, and that they clearly communicate the nature of developmentally appropriate curriculum.* A kindergarten teacher attached notes to children's scribbles, describing the progress evident in control and use of symbols to represent reality. She also copied many experience charts, letters, or anything else the group dictated. She duplicated and sent home many of these materials with each child. Books made by the group also were photocopied and forwarded home. In order to foster an understanding of the curriculum, other teachers sent parents photos of children working together in a group, completed group projects, and tape recordings of children singing and reciting poems.

• *Presentations by teachers at parent meetings to show what the children are learning.* One kindergarten teacher made a presentation at a PTA meeting describing the class's unit on pandas. He made an intriguing display of toy pandas, pictures of the children's visit to the zoo, books read during the panda unit, and examples of children's drawings and stories about pandas. In his talk, the teacher explained how the children became involved in the unit, as well as the concepts about pandas the children had acquired. By juxtaposing drawings and writings from the beginning of the unit with those completed at the end of the unit, he demonstrated the children's growth in literacy and concept development.

When projects involve communication between the preschool and elementary school, the entire community will need to be involved. Using communications media and speaking to community groups and religious organizations can help create a better understanding of developmental continuity throughout a community. Send education reporters from the local press a description of the program, detailing the rationale and issues involved. Show pictures of children interacting with each other and the materials of the school, and identify the specific skills the children gained through these and similar experiences. Documentation can be used to raise public awareness of the program's success.

BOTTOM-UP OR TOP-DOWN

Obviously, teachers are not the only ones who can make changes. Administrators, supervisors, principals, or state departments of education are equally responsible for providing developmental continuity throughout children's early years.

Principals and child care directors can take the lead. First gaining the cooperation of two or three teachers, and then beginning to involve parents and the community, they can initiate developmental continuity throughout an entire school system. Alternately, supervisors can enlist the support of representatives from the child care and preschool community in establishing developmentally continuous programs. Regardless, success depends on securing the commitment of others, and establishing communication with parents and others in the community.

With commitment, information about other programs, definitions of developmental continuity, communication with and involvement of others, and authorization of school administration, a group of people can commence the process of developing a program that responds to children's individual needs and allows for continuous growth.

The changes that such a program requires will depend upon how the school presently functions. Since developmental continuity is more successful when there is evolutionary, rather than revolutionary, change, teachers might start with one idea and experiment with what changes are required in the school organization to achieve a natural flow from preschool through 3rd grade. To actively involve children in their own learning, space arrangement, the daily schedule, and the overall classroom environment all will be affected. Although the initial changes may be small, the curriculum's organization and definition eventually will need revision. If children are to be evaluated on how well they are developing, according to their own pace and style of learning, then new ways of assessing and reporting this growth must be developed. Rapid changes in all these areas are not likely to take place; it is more feasible that small steps in one part will lead to changes in another area.

CHAPTER 3

CONTINUITY OF ORGANIZATION

"Laverne and I are beginning to see some important changes in the children's work and progress," Claudia reports excitedly to Consuela, later that year. "Even better, Valerie's and Paul's parents are helping us explain to other parents what is evolving. The principal is in our classrooms almost daily, encouraging us to try new ideas, and he is telling other teachers about what is happening. The principal is even beginning to suggest some structural and organizational changes he thinks might facilitate our successes. You know, Consuela, it's a lot of work."

"Yes," replies Consuela, "but isn't it up to us to find the most exciting ways for each child to succeed? You are lucky to have found an interested colleague, such a supportive principal, and eager parents so early. I had to change schools before I could make these ideas succeed. Your principal seems to be aware that more steps will need to be taken and is willing to be a part of the change process."

To make changes, teachers do need the support of a system that is willing to make alterations in the structure and organization of the school. While such changes can be achieved in many ways, the important components of the change process are: 1) creating a school-based management team, with all parties represented, that advises, assists, and supports classroom teachers' efforts; 2) restructuring the organization of the kindergarten/primary unit; 3) developing strong links with preschools in order to provide smooth transitions for children entering this school for the first time; and 4) establishing continuous support and communication among teachers, administrators, parents, community agencies, and businesses.

SCHOOL MANAGEMENT TEAM

Creating a school management team made up of parents, teachers, and other school personnel is a typical first step. During the initial phases of structuring developmental continuity, the team may include only a couple of teachers, a principal, and parents. As the program grows, however, the team needs to grow with it. During the program's evaluation, new interests and needs will arise that can be met by representatives from parent groups, other teachers, administrators, members of the child care and preschool community, and/or community agencies and businesses.

In one school, Jim and Felicity, a kindergarten and 1st-grade teacher, respectively, had begun to work together to plan units so that their curriculum would make more sense to their students. Before too long, two of the parents became interested in the units and began trying to generate parent involvement for their projects. Other teachers, sensing the enthusiasm, began to "borrow" their ideas, and soon the principal began to change teachers' meetings to include more planning on a school-wide scale.

While these curriculum changes were being implemented, the children's interest in exploring topics was taking them beyond the classroom and into the community. The teachers had always "taken trips" into the community, but some children wanted to explore more about how certain businesses were run. One of the parents on the team suggested that her boss could help. Indeed he did, and he even garnered some support from his business associates in the chamber of commerce.

The "team" that initially included only Jim and Felicity was growing as more and more people became interested. At this point, the principal decided to form a school management team to coordinate the many activities. Today, teachers in that school often form a small subgroup with parents for planning; they find the support of the management helpful in many ways.

While the purpose and tasks of a management team will evolve, the original tasks are to:

- Facilitate and coordinate the cooperation of classroom staff within the kindergarten/primary unit
- Establish methods of communicating with the child care and preschool community
- Enlist and coordinate the services of other appropriate groups, as children's needs demand
- Assess the success of the process
- Read about and visit other programs and research projects that are organized for developmental continuity.

The school management team, while fostering communication between and among those involved in creating developmental continuity, also serves as a source of support and encouragement for teachers and parents striving to build curriculum that continuously responds to children's development. When teachers' decisions about classroom procedures are in conflict with others and/or with children's apparent needs, the school management team can serve as the arbiter for final decisions. Finally, the team is responsible for coordinating the teachers' goals with those of the child care/preschool community, the local system, and state policies.

State and local school boards set policies to ensure quality education for the children under their jurisdiction. The team's responsibilities would include study of these policies and recommendations for change to address apparent needs. Guidelines for restructuring should first be made within stated policies.

For example, if the local school authorities require that evaluations of children be made using uniform report cards, then the reporting process, at first, will have to fall within these guidelines. However, evaluation procedures using a more developmentally appropriate reporting system should be introduced and shared with parents, other teachers, and administrators. After generating support for the new procedures, the school management team can approach the local school board with a proposal either to allow for an exception to the existing grading system or to examine the current policy with the aim of revising it.

School restructuring must be done in a way that allows continuous opportunities for renewal. As changes are made, part of the team's responsibility would be to assess the communication process, both within and across units and to the larger community. Periodically, the team would determine if the various groups responsible for children's development are adequately represented on the team (SAMPI-Western Michigan University, 2001).

The school management team also plays an important role in professional development. Team members would examine additional training and education available for teachers, administrators, paraprofessionals, parents, and staff of the community agencies serving the school community. Workshops, university coursework, lectures, television productions, books, and articles would be made available, and topics for discussion sessions identified and planned.

The management team also would develop cooperative arrangements with college and university departments of education. Using the Professional Development School (PDS) model (Darling-Hammond, 1994; Teitel & Abdel-Haqq, 2000), teachers and teacher educators collaborate to conduct joint research projects, provide mutually beneficial opportunities for preservice teachers, and explore learning opportunities for children. In a PDS, university professors can become members of the school management team and teachers can participate in curriculum development at the college and university level. Through enhanced collaboration at many levels, both institutions benefit. The school can profit from the expertise of university personnel and, in return, can offer the uni-

versity research opportunities and enhanced experiences for preservice teachers. School-university partnerships also enable university professors to keep in contact with the day-to-day workings of the school and with issues confronting classroom teachers.

RESTRUCTURING THE KINDERGARTEN/PRIMARY UNIT

If each child is to have an initial school experience that allows for a smooth transition from his/her earlier experiences, then some of the traditional ways schools have been organized will need to be changed. It will be necessary to try different methods of grouping, scheduling, promotion, staffing, and reporting in order to break the rigid barriers of age/grade grouping.

GROUPING

A curriculum that responds to children's continuing development depends on a community of learners who progress at their own individual paces across the preschool and primary units (Katz, Evangelou, & Hartman, 1990, p. vii). The unit consists of the children and teachers in the preschool and primary grades for whom the management team is responsible. While the unit will cut across age ranges, this may vary from school to school. The size of the unit, grouping within the unit, and teacher/group arrangement are important considerations.

Size of the Unit. The unit must be small enough so that teaching/learning can be personalized. Although size might vary from school to school, 100 children per unit is a workable figure. A smaller unit allows parents, teachers, and other school personnel to know all members of the unit and to work together as a community.

Grouping Within the Unit. Multiage grouping recognizes that children learn from one another. "In families, villages, settlements, neighborhoods, and even transient settings such as during travel, children imitate, instruct, direct, follow, interrogate, and respond to one another's knowledge, ideas and feelings" (Katz, Evangelou, & Hartman, 1990, p. vii).

The British call multiage classes "family groupings," meaning that, just as in a family, the class includes children of different ages and different expectations are held for each child. Children are usually grouped in ages of 4-5-6, 5-6-7, or 6-7-8. Grouping is flexible; as older children move on to join a new group, younger children come in. With a small number of new children to acclimate to the classroom, teachers and children begin each year with less trauma and adjustment.

Organizing classrooms with multiage groups of children provides greater opportunities for meeting children's individual needs (Chase & Doan, 1996). Children in these groups are believed to benefit from being with both older and younger peers. Younger children benefit from the support of older ones, and older children benefit from helping and teaching younger ones. A 5-year-old, for example, can get help from an older child in figuring out a story sequence, while the older child practices skills of explaining and clarifying.

Chase and Doan (1994) suggest that a successful multiage program should be based on a workshop or center environment; focus on integrated learning, student choice, and responsibility for learning; and foster collaboration among students in a familial atmosphere. They also stress the importance of parent involvement in a multiage classroom. With all the flexibility such a program provides, there is no need for retention in grade or special promotion to the next grade; each child's unique developmental needs can be met by the greater flexibility inherent in multiage groupings.

Same Teacher/Same Group. Allowing the same teacher to stay with her kindergarten class as they proceed into the primary grades is another way of structuring flexibility. In this process, sometimes known as looping, the teacher returns to the earliest grade after completing two or three years with the same group. Relationships between and among children and their teacher are strengthened when they are able to spend several years together. Everyone knows one another and trusts one another. The time usually spent at the beginning of the year becoming acquainted is invested more profitably in building on summer experiences.

Keeping teacher and children together for several years allows teachers to build on children's previous experiences and gives children time to grow. Looping can be especially beneficial to children who are learning English as a second language (Kuball, 1999). Because many children spurt ahead in some skills but lag behind in others, being with the same group over time permits both teacher and children time to meet individual needs. A teacher explained it this way: "At the end of 1st grade, Robert still wasn't reading, and he wasn't much interested in learning, either. On the other hand, his progress in math skills was amazing. But that seemed to happen almost overnight. Robert and I know and trust each other, so we know that we will find the way to help him master reading, which may also seem to happen suddenly."

With this grouping approach, transitions from one grade to the next are smoother, for no time is wasted in getting to know one another. The teacher knows each child and has established relationships with the children's parents (Little & Dacus, 1999). After summer vacation, coming back to school takes on the spirit of a reunion, and resumption of school tasks occurs naturally.

By staying with the same students, teachers are also able to do more with them. A 2nd-grade teacher in Boston, who had stayed with the same group since kindergarten, took the class on a skiing trip to Vermont. She admitted that 2nd-graders usually would not be ready for an overnight trip away from home and parents, but explained that they *were* a family. She knew each child very well, and each child knew and trusted her.

Although having a teacher stay with the same group of children over two or three years has very positive aspects, it is wise to be alert to situations that may prevent this model from working for a group of children or for a single child. Parents also may object to having their child stay with the same teacher, fearing the child may be "stuck" in an unfavorable situation. Before adopting such a plan, the management team would need to have alternative plans for adjusting the arrangement if it does not work, and to communicate such options to the parents (Bellis, 1999). When flexibility is the rule and the goal is for children to be in developmentally appropriate classrooms, then a primary unit may find that certain groups of children function better with a different teacher each year and with a different set of classmates. Also, an individual child might have a better experience the second year with a different teacher, because of personality differences.

Flexible Grouping. Flexible grouping occurs within each classroom. One 3rd-grade classroom had no permanent groupings; groups were formed for specific purposes and projects. When the goals were achieved or the project completed, the groups were reorganized. Children could belong to more than one group at any given time.

For example, during one month, Jennifer joined two friends every Monday morning to discuss their "reading for fun" weekend books. During project time, she and three other classmates experimented with making quicksand in a geographic land area they had simulated. The project took three days to complete. Jennifer was assigned to a third group of four students who were responsible for illustrating their findings, as the entire class examined the moon phases for a month. She and five other students worked together on distinguishing between words beginning with "wh" and those beginning with "w." By the end of the week, all six students successfully mastered the skill. Several times during the day/week, Jennifer participated with the entire class for instruction, discussion, or paper-and-pencil work projects.

With this flexible grouping philosophy, the teacher was able to accommodate diverse interests, learning rates, and styles. Almost always, some assignment would support children's desire to work with special friends. As children expressed interest in special projects or events from their academic studies, they learned to examine problems with students who shared their enthusiasm. At times, children were permitted to work independently on a project of special interest, becoming the class "expert" on that topic. The teacher also carefully assigned groups that would work cooperatively to achieve specific goals. Sometimes, the groups were a deliberate mix; other times, the children were grouped by ability or skill level, depending upon the learning (Fountas & Pinnell, 1996).

SCHEDULING

Providing developmental continuity for all children may require changes in traditional scheduling. In order for children to acquire knowledge by exploring, manipulating, and experimenting, large blocks of time must be designated for activities. Within those large blocks of time a variety of activities and choices may be available. These activities would include both indoor and outdoor events.

For example, Steve's 2nd-grade class schedule usually proceeded in the following manner. The morning began with general group time to discuss the day's plans, establish any necessary routines, and provide any important instructions or information to assist the children as they began their group or individual projects. A reading/writing workshop was followed by a math/science workshop. During these blocks of time, children would select activities or projects to begin, work on, or complete. The activity or project themes were related to science, social studies, literature, and/or mathematics content.

At times, a theme might be related in one workshop area almost exclusively, as when the children were studying different types of fairy tales. For a week during reading/writing workshop time, they investigated similarities and differences in fairy tale formats. At the same time, the science/math workshop focused on investigating the concept of volume, or "how much can different containers hold?" During another week, the entire morning was set aside for one workshop as children were involved in a unit on insects. Groups of children read about, wrote about, and conducted some experiments about insects of their choice.

During workshop time, Steve helped individuals or small groups with reading books, writing their original stories, setting up mathematical or science problems, or developing a particular skill session. As the children worked together, they had time to read by themselves, to each other, or to the teacher; to write; to gather information related to the theme; and/or to work on particular skills. At the end of every morning, Steve called the group together for a summary of the morning's events, a recitation of stories and poems, or group singing.

The afternoon schedule consisted of social studies and personal project time. Special topics of particular interest to the children were selected, with some time allowed for children to work on any "creative" project of their choice or to continue a project started in the morning. One "inventor" made a special doorbell. Another created games for his friends to play. Woodworking, sewing, and craft projects were a few of the activities pursued at this time. Some children read for leisure, others wrote. At one point, a group wrote a play and followed through on its production. Art, music, drama, dance, and physical education activities take place within the classroom, and are taught by specialists outside the classroom. For some of these activities, children met with other children from different classes who had similar interests or special talents. Afternoon dismissal activities included a summary of the day's events and a review of home projects to extend and reinforce learning and/or locate materials for the next day's events.

Such a scheduling plan also permits kindergarten children to move more gradually into a full day. Napping arrangements could be made for those children who still need more quiet or rest time in the afternoon. For children whose parents are at home, arrangements could be made for them to move gradually from a half day of kindergarten to a full day.

In using this scheduling plan for 6-, 7-, and 8-year-olds, the children could gradually begin participating in projects and creative activities outside the classroom with other children from the unit who have similar interests or are of a similar age. The oldest and more developed children also could participate in some experiences with children in the older age units. Such scheduling plans would allow younger children to have the security of only one or two teachers and only one classroom space, while also allowing the older children to gradually experience learning from different instructors and with different peer groups. Thus, children would move into an organizational pattern appropriate for the next stage of development in a continuous and fluid manner.

Some schools have been experimenting with various ways to group children for better instruction (Chase & Doan, 1994, 1996). Some have experimented with mixing 5-, 6-, and 7-year-olds in one class, with the same teacher following the 5-year-olds until they move into the next unit. The schedule allows for half-day kindergarten; one group joins the class in the morning and another group joins them in the afternoon. The curriculum provides concrete hands-on experiences for children, using the project approach and balanced literacy instruction. Science and social studies are integrated into special units that are rotated to avoid duplication. Multiage grouping allows for cooperative learning, peer tutoring, and integrated curriculum, and enables teachers to ensure developmentally appropriate activities (National Association of School Psychologists [NASP], 2002).

PROMOTION

With continuous entry into the kindergarten/primary unit comes continuous exit from the unit; that is, when children reach age 8, or whatever top age the unit is structured for, they are promoted or would move into the next unit. If the middle school unit also is designed for the success of all children, then those children who are not ready to spend the entire day in the middle school structure initially would spend part of the day in the primary unit—much like some kindergarten children who initially spend only half days in the school environment.

Although children learn and develop in different ways and at varying rates, there are some benchmarks for the next stage/age. If movement is fluid and continuous, then promotion into the next stage should be natural, with no expectation that all children will have the same knowledge, skill development, or social/emotional development. There are expectations, however, that all children will have learned fundamental reading, computational, and problem-solving skills. They also will have learned fundamental skills for working/interacting with others, operating independently, and responding in an emotionally appropriate manner.

Retention and transitional classrooms, with the negative aspects that too often result in unfortunate labeling and early tracking of children, would be eliminated (NASP, 2002). Children who were not able to move full time into the next unit, however, might spend part of their day in the primary unit, working on appropriate intellectual, social, or physical tasks that help them make a smooth transition into the middle school unit.

CLASS SIZE

The National Education Association (2001), in accordance with recent research, has made the following recommendations concerning child/adult ratios and maximum class size:

- For 3-, 4-, 5-year-olds: a ratio of 2 adults to 20 children, with a maximum class size of 20
- For 6-, 7-, 8-year-olds: a ratio of 1 adult to 15 children, with a maximum class size of 20

Simply reducing class size will not make a difference, unless the strategies used in the classroom provide for individualization, the children are able to learn through hands-on experiences, and there are opportunities for social interaction with other children, other adults, and materials.

With freedom of activity and children initiating and directing their own learning, larger class sizes can only hinder flexibility of scheduling, multiage groupings, and flexibility of grouping. Most important, larger classes limit opportunities for productive child-to-child and adult-to-child interactions.

STAFFING OF THE CLASSROOM

In each classroom across the kindergarten/primary units, there should be a teacher and a paraprofessional who are primarily responsible for the child's educational experiences. If the educational needs of all children are to be met, however, the child's physical welfare, social/emotional development, and moral development also will need to be supported.

With flexible scheduling and grouping patterns, children may, at times, be engaged in activities under the supervision of other teachers, parents, specialists, administrators, social workers, or community personnel. In a school where the developmental needs of children are met in a continuous manner, this additional support should not be segmented, but rather should be part of the total classroom program. For example, children who need a quiet space and a single adult for specific purposes would be able to receive such support according to their need, rather than at the convenience of adult time schedules. Children who are able to function within the classroom would not be pulled away from productive classroom activities, but would receive additional support within the classroom context.

REPORTING PROGRESS

A different procedure is needed to report children's progress. The current practice of reporting children's learning by comparing the standardized tests scores of one group with those of another group is contrary to the notion of different growth patterns and rates. While children, parents, and society at large have a right to know how the schools are doing, reporting standardized test scores does little to inform parents or the community about each child's progress.

More informative reports of children's progress are based on observations, interviews, and collections of children's work. If children are involved in mapping their own progress, they, like their parents, will be aware of their increasing knowledge and skills. Charting children's growth and accomplishments through observations and interviews illustrates their progression to the next stage of development and achievement more accurately than standardized test scores. If progression is not evident, then these methods also give a better indication as to what steps might be taken to ensure positive growth.

According to Goodlad (1984), reorganizing schools would give teachers and children a greater opportunity for

a continuous assessment of each child's progress as a thinking, social, reasonably self-assured person. The vertical organization of each unit of 100 children or less who stay together with approximately the same team of teachers over a period of four years facilitates a developmental view of the child and provides the necessary time for assessment, diagnosis, and relatively long-term interventions. The availability of a highly trained head teacher in each unit adds to the likelihood of sound diagnoses and subsequent programmatic adjustments. Much can be done to redesign the program of a 6-year-old appearing to be having difficulties so that progress in all areas is proceeding nicely by the age of 8. The present choppy, graded organization of schools is not conducive to the identification and redirection of developmental deficiencies and irregularities. (pp. 333-334)

ORGANIZING MATERIALS, SUPPLIES, AND PEOPLE

School systems must find ways to organize materials, supplies, and people. A central materials room within a school unit, as well as space within each classroom, is helpful. Expensive materials that are not needed in each classroom every day would be rotated among classes when interests or needs arise. A transportation unit might require extra large or unit blocks and specific materials for road construction. Special materials might be required to build a harbor in the sand table. Teachers would not need these materials every day, but could reserve them for use during the transportation unit.

Most schools have media centers with special thematic material, as well as libraries of good children's literature. Teachers also use the public libraries to enhance their book and material selections around certain themes. A central materials room in each unit would provide some extra books and stories in basal readers marked for difficulty level, unit themes, and interest, as well as reference lists and materials lists.

Resource specialists also need to be available for teachers. A system moving toward developmental continuity would have teachers meet with all music, art, physical education, and other resource teachers and personnel to coordinate the programmatic need and changes in the kindergarten/primary unit. The management team would help teachers, the principal, and parents determine how best to work together with the resource persons.

STRONG LINKS WITH PRESCHOOLS

Even if children are from the same community, they are likely to have had very different experiences before entering school. If children are to make comfortable transitions to their new school, then teachers and caregivers need to understand their students' prior experiences. Consequently, communication between the management team and the area preschool and child care communities is essential.

The management team at the school would take responsibility for establishing links between the preschool and primary grades. Child care professionals, teachers, parents, and administrators can cooperate in a number of ways to structure smooth transitions for children from their preschool or child care experience to the kindergarten and primary grades. This cooperation involves:

- Communicating with parents and other teachers
- Preparing children for the transition
- Developing compatible administrative practices.

COMMUNICATING WITH PARENTS AND OTHER TEACHERS

Many parents are actively involved in their children's preschool and child care experiences. They often see and talk with their child's teachers on a daily basis, as well as volunteer in the classroom and serve on advisory and policy boards. Parents need to be encouraged to continue this involvement as their children move into the elementary school.

Providing linkages with the child care center or preschool where parents have placed their children requires different approaches to establishing communication. It does not mean that all schools will be involved initially as kindergarten and primary school teachers begin the process. A parent, a child care professional, and a teacher can begin the communication process with the intent of providing smoother transitions from one setting to another. As good communication patterns and smoother transitions are provided for a few of the children, other people can be involved. As adults become more adept at making "schools fit the child" rather than making the "child fit the school," different models and approaches to the process will emerge.

The communication process can begin with arranging home and school visits, organizing meetings, sharing newsletters, serving on boards, and sharing records.

Home and School Visits. Making home visits is one of the ways teachers can get to know parents better. Although the potential of such visits is yet to be fully realized, home visits provide extensive information about children and how they function in a family setting. It is also true that when teachers and child care workers arrange visits to each other's work place, they gain a greater understanding of children's experiences in both settings. From such visits, each would begin to understand the child's environment and how the structure of each day progresses. As an added benefit, each can observe how children function in a different environment. Teachers can learn how a child who will be entering their class relates with other children and adults. Child care staff can observe how their children are adapting to the new situation, as well as how other children seem to adapt. Educators can ask themselves what seems to be working well for the children and what might be done differently when a child is having a difficult time.

Organized Meetings. Times should be arranged for child care staff and teachers to meet and discuss their ideas, philosophies, and goals for providing the best possible education opportunities for the children with whom they work. These meetings are more productive when they have a purpose and goal. Various meeting formats can be used, depending on the people involved. Informal meetings provide opportunities for open discussion about specific issues; at more formal meetings a speaker may discuss some current topic of mutual concern. It might be appropriate for teachers and child care professionals to attend workshops and/or take courses together, to increase their understanding about child development and appropriate practices. At the very least, knowledge of available workshops and courses should be shared with all.

Sharing Newsletters. Schools and child care centers often send newsletters home to parents as a means of maintaining contact and communication. These letters can be exchanged between the elementary school and the child care and preschool programs, as well. By exchanging newsletters, the personnel in each setting will be aware of the information that each provides to parents and the special events they hold. These newsletters often include articles, reviews or summaries of books, and notices of upcoming events. Gaining knowledge about the experiences provided for children in various settings can help others extend these experiences and prepare children for future events.

Board Members. The composition of the board can be an important factor in building developmental continuity. Kindergarten teachers should be invited to sit on preschool or child care advisory boards, while preschool teachers can be involved in the policy advisory boards or the management teams of the elementary school. Each group benefits, as other advisory board members will then be up-to-date on what is happening in the various classrooms, and teachers will play a role in board decisions.

Joint Records. In order to provide appropriate curricula for children, teachers need to exchange pertinent information about children's growth. Preschool staff and the school management team might cooperate in transferring records from the preschool to the kindergarten or in developing joint records that follow children across the preschool and primary grades. Preschool teachers also

could write letters to the receiving schools in the spring, listing the names of incoming children and communicating information about their preschool program.

Home/school journaling is another way to strengthen communication between home and school (Bersani & Jarjoura, 2002). With this approach, families receive a notebook with their children's pictures on the front cover. The notebook, or journal, circulates between home and school, with families and teachers writing down their perceptions about children's adjustments to school, as well as their accomplishments or problems, and responding to the other's comments.

PREPARING CHILDREN

With open communication between the elementary school and feeder preschools and child care centers, teachers from both settings can design unique ways to prepare children for their transition into the kindergarten. One kindergarten class made a booklet for each child in the feeder preschool. In this booklet, the children dictated and illustrated the things they had done in kindergarten and described what they had learned. In another child care classroom, children who had moved on to kindergarten returned to their former classroom and told the younger children about their experiences in the "big" school.

In another school, the management team made a video of their school day. They started with the ride to school, and followed a child throughout the school day. They also interviewed kindergarten children, who described what they liked best about kindergarten and explained how kindergarten was different from preschool. Copies of the video were sent to the four feeder preschools.

Preschool teachers have found that children's enactment of going to kindergarten is helpful in smoothing the transition. Children can take turns pretending to ride the bus, sitting and listening to a story, and eating lunch in a cafeteria.

One preschool teacher created puppets to represent the kindergarten teacher, the principal, a cafeteria worker, and some kindergarten children. Using the puppet stage the group had often used in the past, she encouraged the children to play "going to kindergarten." She used one of the puppets herself to correct misconceptions, give feedback, and keep the play moving.

One teacher, concerned that her children wouldn't know how to adapt to some of the routines of the big school, took a few children at a time to visit the school. The kindergarten children served as guides to the visitors as they toured the whole school; met the principal, the cafeteria workers, and others in the school; and visited in the classroom. The kindergartners sat with their guests for snack time and played with them at recess. Upon their return, the preschoolers discussed their feelings and role-played situations that concerned them.

In another school district, personnel from the public school made field trips to the community preschools. The librarian, cook, custodian, and representatives from the kindergarten and primary grades visited area preschools in order to introduce themselves and their school to the children. Some schools even have arranged for children to ride the school bus, with their parents, from the preschool to the elementary school.

Children who have never been to preschool or child care should be identified by the management team so that both parents and children can be invited to share some of the same experiences.

SUPPORT AND COMMUNICATION LINKS TO THE COMMUNITY

Society today differs drastically from the culture of the early 1900s, when present school organizations were formed. The family continues to be the mainstay for any youngster; however, the family units today differ dramatically from the nuclear and extended family units prevalent during the early 1900s.

This means that the traditional models of parent/school relationships are probably not sufficient to educate today's children to become socially responsible, mentally and physically competent, and motivated to become productive citizens.

Large school systems have been organized in ways that take a sense of ownership and responsibility away from parents and others from the local community. Even though community agencies offer a variety of support systems for parents and children, this support is often fragmented; therefore, children are not served as well as they might be through a more cohesive system.

Businesses are beginning to recognize that they have a real stake in the education of tomorrow's citizens. A prosperous economy depends upon a better educated and adaptable work force. Yet the services or benefits that could accrue from businesses' involvement in schools remain largely unfulfilled for two reasons: 1) the results are not immediate or readily assessed in quantitative ways and 2) the school's goals and businesses' goals are not compatible.

Furthermore, as *Children of 2010* (Washington & Andrews, 1999) points out, today's children bring diverse backgrounds and experiences to the classroom. In Los Angeles, there are over 100 ethnic groups speaking 70 languages. It is predicted that by the year 2010, the majority of children in California, New York, and Florida will be of color. Children bring different intellectual skills to the classroom and represent a wide variety of family structures, bringing with them another type of "cultural capital" into classrooms. If these patterns are understood and accepted, greater school success for all will be achieved.

Some children have been exposed to more extensive family and community experiences than have others. These experiences require them to adapt their language patterns to different social situations. These children already know that ways of talking that are acceptable to one group need to be altered when talking to someone else. They have had more opportunities to hear siblings, parents, and significant adults adapt their own language to different situations; for example, their mother uses a rather simple language pattern to speak to the baby, but when talking to the father uses more complex sentences, and when explaining a situation to the minister she uses more formal speech. These children are expected to respond in increasingly more complex ways.

In all homes, children observe written language; however, the emphasis on using written language as a means of communicating varies widely. Many of our "at-risk" students are from cultural groups that place more emphasis on oral language and use written language in more restricted ways. Yet, the focus on written language is increasing in early schooling. Thus, children whose home culture does not focus on written language are at a disadvantage.

Regardless of background, children who are academically successful have participated in activities beyond the school and home that demand a complex repertoire of oral and written skills. They may have participated in preschool story hours at the library. They may have belonged to various community organizations (such as scouting), participated in athletics, taken specialized lessons (such as art, music, drama), or even participated in work-related activities. Successful participation in these beyond-school experiences provides them with skills to become more language proficient, more self-assured, and more physically and socially competent. These competencies usually support them as they address the academic demands of formal schooling. Since such services already exist for some children, schools are becoming more like brokers of multiple services instead of delivering these services (Head Start-Public School Transition Demonstration [HSPSTD], 1999).

FAMILY SUPPORT

Schools traditionally have considered establishing good home/school relationships as part of their responsibility. With changing societal demands on parents, however, this task becomes more difficult. When school personnel give the impression that children are failing because "something is wrong with the child or the parent," then adversarial roles develop. Viewing their role as a "broker" will allow school management teams to accept the responsibility to break down these barriers and build bridges. Consequently, all parents will understand the importance of being involved in their children's growth and development, and recognize the contributions they can make toward their children's education. Just as children have different levels of needs, parents' ability to respond to their children's needs also varies.

Many successful programs for parent involvement exist (Brandt, 1989; Galen, 1991; Vandergrift & Greene, 1992). Part of the management team's task would be to keep informed about these programs and model efforts for increasing parent involvement, based on other success stories. The team would be able to articulate the goals of developmental continuity: that all children will achieve academic, social, and physical skills, even though the rate of progress may not be the same for all children, nor will progress always be in even patterns. Goals should be set for parent involvement, with the ultimate goal being to convince all parents that success for their children requires their active support and cooperation, even if the outward manifestation of that support varies. Then, the task of the team would be to determine what beginning steps need to be taken and how to assess the progress that is being made towards achieving the ultimate goal.

COMMUNITY SUPPORT

Community support might begin with one classroom, one or two teachers, a few parents, and a supportive administrator. As the team approaches the task of being a "broker," the success of developmental continuity will ultimately depend upon children receiving the benefits of a community that cooperates to provide appropriate expertise and services. At some point, the management team will need to incorporate a "community resource" person who can determine how, when, and where health, library, tutoring, counseling, athletic, artistic, social, and other appropriate services can be provided to all the children in the school.

Various innovative community support programs are in operation today. At times, the project is all-encompassing, as in the Yale Child Welfare Research Program (Comer, Ben-Avie, Haynes, & Joyner, 1999). Nevertheless, many schools need assistance from diverse community agencies. For example, universities are supporting college students as they tutor, act as mentors, and sponsor clubs for the children in a particular school or group of schools. Universities often offer special seminars to the student-tutors so that they can examine the impact of the services they render.

Enthusiasm and commitment can start the process of community support; however, as the team expands, members will need to determine what is achievable as well as profitable in order to ensure the success of the children in school.

BUSINESS SUPPORT

Businesses have successfully contributed to the schools in their community in various ways. Some have contributed equipment (such as computers) or money to schools to support specific changes in curriculum or major school reform. Some have cooperated in developing full-day kindergarten programs as a part of their child care services. In other instances, businesses have provided incentive programs for students to get better grades or to achieve on certain tasks, such as reading a number of books and sharing them with parents and teachers. Not all of the ven-

tures have been successful; those planned by administrators and business leaders without regard to those who must implement the project or who will be recipients of their efforts are less likely to succeed. For a school concerned with implementing programs in a fashion consistent with developmentally appropriate practices, business partnerships must be developed out of the needs of the particular students in the schools. The school management team would assess not only the students' needs but also a business's potential for providing that need.

It is best to initiate business support for schools by becoming acquainted with the institutions involved. Team members should visit the place of business in the spirit of "what can we do for each other." Business people would visit the schools, or even volunteer, to become better acquainted with the goals of the school, the staff and students, and current methods of education. In this way, they would gain better insights into the schooling process. This reciprocity would equip those involved with better knowledge of the resources, ideas, and level of commitment that each party could bring to the partnership. Roles and resources might change from year to year, depending on the students' needs and the commitment of the businesses. MacDowell (1989) offers some general guidelines for establishing positive school/business partnerships:

- Select those areas of the curriculum or unit that appeal to the business, or where there is some expertise within the company
- Make sure the goals of the school and of the company are compatible
- Familiarize the company with the realities of schooling
- Make sure that the success of the involvement is measured by how well it matches the appropriate goals for student growth
- Consider a diverse type of involvement for the company, aside from contributions of money and materials. (p. 9)

With successful partnerships, the school management teams eventually should include a representative from the business community. This practice can serve as a reminder to influential leaders about the importance of providing quality education for all children.

Most schools will have to make substantial changes to provide developmental continuity for tomorrow's children. Although it is not possible for a single teacher to bring about the kinds of changes that are required, a teacher committed to improving education for all children can seek out other like-minded teachers, parents, and administrators and begin to experiment with changes in school organization. A small management team can restructure a single kindergarten/primary unit, organize links with preschools and child care centers whose children will be a part of the unit, establish strong communication with those involved initially—teachers, administrators, and parents—and later establish ties with community agencies and businesses. When change results in children achieving greater success and feeling more positively toward school, then more people can be encouraged to participate.

CHAPTER 4

CONTINUITY OF CURRICULUM

The three friends gather once again to discuss their mutual interest in developmental continuity. "Laverne, are you feeling the pressure to get children reading the way I am with my kindergartners?" asks Claudia. "I sure am," Laverne replies. "Head Start has a new literacy initiative to make certain the children are getting lots of experience with books and print. We're even supposed to be helping them learn letters and sounds. For me, it's more important than ever that I keep my program appropriate in light of these expectations." Claudia nods and, turning to Consuela, says, "Tell us more about what's going on in your classroom. If you're meeting the increased demands of your system and are still meeting your children's needs, we can see why you get so excited about your developmental curriculum!"

"It's always exciting to see change in the classroom," replies Consuela. "Children get so involved in their projects, they ask very stimulating questions, and I find that I'm constantly learning new things myself. It is hard work! I'm always planning, thinking about what new materials children may need to continue their investigations, learning about each child and his/her growth. I find myself worrying when Jenny doesn't grasp the concept that containers hold the same amount in spite of their shape, when the rest of the class has long ago comprehended it. But then, I'm dazzled when suddenly she exclaims, 'Wow, every one of these containers holds three of whatever I put in. They must really be the same size.' I feel more invigorated in my teaching than I have in years."

"But don't you worry about covering your district's content standards and making certain that the children are meeting the required performance outcomes?" Claudia wonders. "With all the emphasis on standards-based learning these days, there is a great deal of pressure for children to learn more if we expect them to succeed. All the excitement we feel about them learning new things in a new way may not be enough in today's test-driven school environment."

"Believe me, you'll see children learning the required skills," answers Consuela. "In fact, I am always checking to make sure that what we're doing in the classroom is in line with the standards. I've discovered the children are meeting the outcomes and lots more besides. Let me tell you about last week," she adds. "We've been focusing on developing our observation skills, so the children have been bringing in things, looking at them, comparing how they looked to the naked eye and then how they looked under the microscope. Monday, several of them brought in leaves because they found them so colorful. I may not see anything new in fall leaves, but the children haven't seen as many falls as I have, and they love collecting the leaves. When you think about it, fall is still new to them. It's new and familiar at the same time. Maybe it's the familiarity of working with leaves that enables children to feel secure enough to risk learning something new like graphing.

"At first they began to make comparisons like they had been doing, and we listed all sorts of characteristics they observed: colors, pointed or round ends, numbers of points a leaf had, short or long leaves. We identified those the children knew the names of, and the children volunteered to go to the library and find books about trees. Other children volunteered to try to find some different leaves to bring into the classroom.

"That afternoon the children began to categorize the leaves according to the characteristics; during math, since we had begun a graphing unit, children formed groups to make graphs of the different characteristics, labeling them large to small, pointed to round, light to dark.

"As the project unfolded, children began to identify their leaves with trees, using the books we had found in the library. A walk around the schoolyard helped us to identify which trees grew near the school and to compare the pictured tree to the real tree. Children continued to bring leaves from home or a walk in the woods with their parents. During group times, children shared what they were discovering and posed questions of what else they could find out. I read the poem *Trees* by Joyce Kilmer and a few of the poems in a beautiful collection with amazing photographs called *Leaf by Leaf: Autumn Poems* (Rogasky, 2001). During writing time, we first composed a poem together about leaves, and then the children wrote their own poems or stories. Some children illustrated their work; others chose to paint a picture to express what they learned about trees. I am collecting their work into a book that they will be able to borrow and take home to share with their parents. The children have been enjoying a book I read aloud at the beginning of our study, *Fall Leaves Fall* (Hall, 2000). It has everything in it that my children have been enjoying doing with leaves: collecting, comparing, labeling, and making pictures with them. Best of all, it's at a reading level that allows every child in the class to read it independently. Of course, I have gathered a large collection of books about leaves and trees from the library, and the children have been sharing some of their own books as well.

"The children have already started to summarize and document what they have learned from their study of leaves. This summary helps me keep track of the individual children's learning. As children are discovering new trees, the focus has begun to center on what kinds of trees exist, and where. With the children's continuing interest, I'm eager to see where their questions will take them. With all the focus on literacy instruction these days, it can be hard to make room in the daily schedule for science and social studies; by integrating the curriculum around a topic, however, we can do it all.

"Just sharing this experience with you makes me realize how much more my children learned last week than if I had merely proceeded with the next story in the reading anthology or relied solely on the science textbook. The children counted and measured leaves; they made and gained meaning from a bar graph. Each selected at least one book to read, which they shared in small groups. In reading, we are focusing on how authors indicate setting. Among other things, the children noted where the trees were found and how the authors showed that in their books. In writing their poems and stories, many were able to use different and creative descriptors. Reading their work led to a great mini-lesson on adjectives and how such words help to make pictures appear more clearly in the minds of our readers.

"They also gained a lot of experience working together in groups. The power of this informal give-and-take communication is immense. While working on group projects, children find it necessary to make their ideas clear to others, and they must learn to listen to others' ideas as well. Of course, this doesn't happen naturally. From the beginning of the school year, we work hard to develop a classroom community.

"You know, taking time to actually document in writing what the children have done has uncovered something else they learned. To find the names of the trees and other information they wanted, I realized that the librarian, or in some cases the parents, had showed them how to use a table of contents and an index. I am going to follow up on that skill and add it to my next lesson plan. I need to know which ones are skilled in this area and which ones will need more guidance from me.

"Using a developmental curriculum makes it necessary for me to really know and understand the content standards and performance expectations of the school. I have to be able to demonstrate that my children are mastering the required skills within the integrated curricular approach I'm using. I start with what the children find meaningful, consider their needs and abilities, and work with them to develop activities that foster their learning. With all the current emphasis on literacy, I always build in lots of opportunities for reading and writing. And when children are interested in a topic, they are eager to read and write about it! I begin my planning with the children in mind—knowledge of them helps me decide what skills I'll introduce, which ones I'll ask the children to practice, and how and when."

I CREATING MEANINGFUL CURRICULUM

In order to create meaningful curriculum for children, teachers need to understand the societal expectations concerning the function of schooling, as well as what is appropriate instruction for children. Each school and each school system has standards and expected outcomes for children's achievement, which are usually developed by state departments of education, school boards, groups of teachers within a system, or parent groups. National professional organizations also have developed standards for children in grades kindergarten through 12 in all subject areas. Content standards specify what children should be able to do, and performance standards gauge the level of competence a child has reached. These expectations must be in line with children's developmental levels if quality educational experiences for all children are to be provided.

A school's or a system's expectations, when stated as appropriate standards and outcomes for children's learning, offer teachers a solid framework for curriculum planning. Rather than limiting teacher or child choice, such a framework ensures that all children will have equal access to quality educational experiences. By following and adhering to appropriate expectations of the school and striving to change inappropriate ones, teachers know that their curriculum will: 1) reflect the values of the community, 2) provide all children with the same curriculum opportunities, and 3) offer a balance of goals and objectives from each subject area discipline.

"Honestly," said Consuela, "I do follow the standards of the school as I plan my curriculum. It is just that if I followed these expectations exactly as stated, they would have little meaning to the children I teach. Each teacher needs to figure out how to make the expectations of the school meaningful to her individual group of children, and to each child within the group."

Meaningfulness is all-important. There doesn't seem to be any doubt about the need for teachers to make the things they teach meaningful to children. "Research [demonstrates] that the more meaningful, the more deeply or elaborately processed, the more situated in context and personal knowledge an event is, the more readily it is understood, learned, and remembered" (Iran-Nejad, McKeachie, & Berliner, 1990, p. 511).

Curriculum that continually responds to the children and holds meaning for them may, as Consuela suggested, begin with the children themselves. It probably is more accurate, however, to say that a curriculum with developmental continuity begins with the teacher. A teacher needs to be a specialist in:

- *Understanding children*—their individual growth, development, interests, needs, and learning styles
- *Understanding the environment in which children live*—their physical environment and also the culture of their home, neighborhood, and community
- *Understanding curriculum content*—being interested in and knowledgeable about every discipline, with special expertise in at least one subject area
- *Understanding the process of planning*—organizing and reorganizing classroom space, schedules, and particular content that is appropriate for all the children.

UNDERSTANDING CHILDREN

In her unit on fall leaves, Consuela illustrated how the expectations of the school could be made meaningful to her children. She was able to respond to children's interest in fall leaves and, at the same time, foster achievement of the school's goals because she knew her children. Consuela's understanding included: 1) knowledge of children's typical growth and development, and 2) an understanding of each individual child's developmental level.

TYPICAL GROWTH AND DEVELOPMENT

Teachers plan appropriate curriculum that follows children's continuous growth by recognizing the universal, predictable sequences of growth and change that occur during the first years of life (Bredekamp & Copple, 1997, p. 9). Teachers also understand that children of the same age may have had very different early opportunities for learning, which may have affected their development. Increasingly, too, children with special needs are placed in the regular classroom, and so teachers must create early childhood programs that enable all children to flourish. Whether a child is disabled (unable to do or has difficulty doing one or more specific tasks), at risk (experiencing a developmental delay due to negative genetic or environmental factors), or gifted (demonstrating excellence in an aspect of development well beyond most children of the same age), teachers must provide appropriate curriculum for everyone (Henniger, 2002). By using their knowledge of typical growth and development, and of each individual child's experiences and learning needs, teachers can plan curriculum that includes concrete materials, direct experiences, and hands-on activities to challenge children, yet respect their unique way of learning.

Three- and 4-year-olds. Teachers of preschoolers must plan a great deal of active learning into the curriculum, since they know that 3- and 4-year-olds have an extremely high energy level and are constantly refining their gross and fine motor skills. They plan short group times that involve a lot of spontaneous talk and discussion and opportunities to move. They choose active songs, in which children are encouraged to move their entire bodies to the rhythm of the words or the music. They select stories and poems that involve children in motion, encourage them to repeat familiar phrases, or say the character's words. For those 3- and 4-year-olds who are ready for longer stories, the teacher plans time when he/she or another adult can read to one, two, or even three children, permitting those who lose interest to move on to another activity. As stories are read aloud, young children come to know a lot about how to handle and enjoy books. They learn that letters can be named, print carries meaning, and that drawing and writing are different. Through active, engaging activities with books and music, 3- and 4-year-olds can learn to recognize their names in print and those of their friends, can clap the syllables of these names, and begin to recognize important letters (like those in their names or favorites stories) in various contexts.

Centers of interest offer 3- and 4-year-olds opportunities to manipulate their environment, make discoveries, and satisfy their curiosity. As they work in centers of interest, 3- and 4-year-olds are happy to play side-by-side with others; they are loving and cooperative one minute, bossy and resistant the next. Working together or alone in the block area, house corner, computer station, writing center, art area, or other centers of interest gives the children varied experiences in many different areas of development and learning. Children's social and emotional development is enhanced as they learn the give-and-take of playing with others. Oral language, literacy, the arts, social studies, science, and math all can be facilitated through the interesting materials and activities provided in interest centers. When 3s and 4s express an interest in learning more about a particular topic, the centers can be further enriched to reflect a theme of study.

Five- and 6-year-olds. Five- and 6-year-olds are expanding their knowledge of the world and the universe. They have built vocabulary and discovered that words can have more than one meaning. Not only are they physically active, 5- and 6-year-olds' bodies are developing rapidly. They are generally quite agile, and now have more control over their bodies. Their fine muscle control has developed enough so they can draw representational pictures and can write, albeit not on a line or in a restricted space. Letters are not uniform, and reversals are still common.

Cognitively, 5- and 6-year-olds are ready to acquire a great many intellectual and academic skills. They become aware that symbols have meaning and that a technique exists for figuring out these symbols. Group discussions can take place, and children can participate in planning activities. Fives can listen to a visitor, ask questions, and summarize what took place during the visit.

Five- and 6-year-olds need many opportunities to hear stories read aloud and to participate in shared reading of big books, charts, and stories they have helped compose. These encounters help them refine their understanding of print concepts and to develop phonemic awareness—the ability to manipulate the sounds of language through print. Children can write stories using their own forms of spelling, grammar, and punctuation.

As their social interaction skills develop, 5- and 6-year-olds form friendships and are able to move in and out of small groups. They usually are cooperative and helpful, and they can assume responsibility for small tasks to help maintain their homes and classrooms. Five-year-olds are beginning to express their feelings in socially accepted ways, are expanding their understanding of their emotions, and are able to attach words to express them. Six-year-olds, on the other hand, may seem to be in emotional ferment, capable of wild outbursts of joy and sudden shifts to tears. As their awareness of their emotions grows, they are sometimes alarmed and puzzled by their conflicting feelings.

Seven- to 9-year-olds. In the later primary years, between 7 and 9 years of age, children are expanding their horizons. They are still asking for help or advice, but may take greater personal learning risks, especially if the environment provides safety for their developing self-esteem. This age group "delights in cooperative projects, activities, and tasks" (Wood, 1994, p. 53). Continuing to be curious about their world, they are able to enter into adult-like conversations at times.

By age 7 most children will be successful in reading simple texts, and some will be well on their way to fluency. Still, opportunities need to be provided for those children who cannot yet read, and teachers must find ways to help these children discover the process of decoding text, building on their understanding of sound/letter relationships to derive meaning.

Children's written stories become more elaborate as they explore more sophisticated social studies, science, and math concepts. They can revise their writing to improve their ideas, spelling, and grammar, if such tasks are introduced gradually and with direction and purpose.

Many 8- and 9-year-olds are moving from preoperational thought to concrete operations. They hypothesize and figure out complex relationships. They sustain interest in projects over several weeks. Most children understand how characters in a story change as a result of the described events, although the time frameworks within a story may be difficult for some children to grasp. Peer relationships are important and, if they have had prior experiences working in groups, most children can participate in group projects with minimal supervision. Eights and 9s can take on more responsibility for their own learning, and so they should be given opportunities to make decisions about how to do things and be allowed to see the consequences of those decisions.

USING KNOWLEDGE OF
TYPICAL GROWTH AND DEVELOPMENT

Preschool and primary children are just beginning a lifetime of learning. Teachers must continually remind themselves that meaningful curriculum also is age-appropriate. Inappropriate curriculum often leads to confusion and misconceptions.

For example, in one 5-year-old group, several of the children's families had new babies. Two mothers brought their babies to visit the class, and the teacher read books on birth and growth. The children were fascinated, and expressed much interest in the books and in relating how the real babies were like those in the stories. Then, the teacher used a strategy she had heard about from a friend who teaches high school. Following the babies' visit, the teacher presented each child with a raw egg in the shell; half of the eggs were marked with a blue dot and the other half with a pink dot. The teacher explained to the children that they were to take care of their eggs all day, just as mothers and fathers take care of their babies all day. She said, "Babies need a lot of care. It's a big responsibility to care for a baby. This egg is like your baby. If you desert it, the baby may be hurt." The rest of the day was a disaster.

The children went off to work in centers, carrying their eggs. A group building with blocks soon tired of the eggs, and so they put them in their cubbies. Later, many of the children were dismayed to discover their eggs had broken. Some children had shoved other objects into the cubbies, forgetting about the eggs. A visitor asked one girl, who was seated alone at a table, what she was doing, and she said, "I don't know, but I know it takes a lot of eggs to make a baby."

The teacher had thought the strategy would teach her students how much care babies require. Clearly, however, the activity was far too abstract for young children.

The curriculum in this classroom on that day was meaningless to the children because the content was age-inappropriate. Five-year-olds, still needing the care of adults, are only beginning to understand how they can care and thus be responsible for someone else. Helping them design a schedule for feeding a classroom animal would be a more age-appropriate way of teaching them this concept. Certainly, the children did not have the cognitive maturity to understand that an egg represented, or was a symbol for, a real baby.

Activities that are too simplistic can be equally disastrous, resulting in horseplay and wasted classroom time. In one classroom of 8-year-olds, for example, the teacher spread shaving cream on the top of the children's desks and directed them to practice cursive writing with their fingertips. "Everyone write, 'The cat in the hat is on the mat' in your shaving cream," the teacher directed. The children messed around for a minute or two and then began to spread shaving cream on one another. When students were asked why they had shaving cream to write in, one of the children said, "Oh, Ms. Smith thinks we have to feel everything."

Feeling the movement of cursive writing in shaving cream was a meaningless experience for these 8-year-olds. Had they been introduced to writing in shaving cream at age 6, the activity might have had more meaning. Eight-year-olds, however, want and need to be challenged and to perfect their skills; therefore, writing in shaving cream was age-inappropriate.

To check whether an activity or content is age-appropriate, Spodek (1977) suggested teachers might ask themselves the following questions:

- Why is this activity, content, and experience worthwhile?
- Why is it important now?
- Would children gain this skill or learn this concept with ease and efficiency if presented to them later in their schooling?
- What prior knowledge do children need in order to master this skill?
- Does this activity offer children a challenge? Is the challenge one they can successfully meet?

Children's Interests. Teachers can more capably select, plan, and implement meaningful curriculum when they use children's interests as a guide. Research shows that when children are interested in something, learning not only has more meaning, it also can accrue long-term benefits for children's mastery of language, reading, and math-

ematical skills (Helm & Katz, 2001).

Of course, most children are interested in learning about themselves, others, and their world. Interests follow patterns of typical growth and development. For example, many 4- and 5-year-olds are interested in issues related to strength and power. They use self-constructed pretend weapons, which help them to feel stronger and more powerful. Yet, most teachers and parents have concerns about allowing children to use weapons in the classroom. Nevertheless, weapons play is prevalent for this age.

One teacher following the Project Approach (Katz & Chard, 2000) in her kindergarten classroom recognized and accepted her children's natural interest in power and weapons. During a study of medieval times, which had emerged from the children's interest in kings, queens, and knights (Scully, Howell, & Corbey-Scullen, 2000), she helped the children develop a "knight training school." The children created cardboard and foil swords and learned the etiquette of fencing, which included bowing, shaking hands, and taking turns. They practiced duels in a designated field under teacher supervision. Weapons play became part of the children's larger interest in creating a castle and holding royal court. Within the rich possibilities of a topic that accommodated a wide variety of interests, weapons play was facilitated in an appropriate way (Carlsson-Paige, 1990, 1995).

Six-year-olds, in the stage Erik Erikson called *industry*, are interested in doing, building, and constructing. A 1st-grade teacher arranged for the children to create a class quilt (Helm, Huebner, & Long, 2000). She initiated the project by sending out surveys to gauge families' interest in the study. After reading and discussing several stories about quilting, the children developed a list of their questions about quilts. They generated a web to record all the things they already knew about quilts, and then began to plan the kind of quilt they wanted to construct as a class. Children brought in quilts from home and gave oral presentations about what the quilts meant to their families. Other children wrote letters to local quilt groups, seeking advice. Some began to create paper squares and patterns. A local quiltmaker agreed to serve as an expert consultant and helped the children draw up plans. Committees of children were organized to determine what materials would be necessary, and at what cost. Other committees were created for fundraising and for trips to the fabric store to purchase the materials. Work started, and children were engaged in constant measuring and re-measuring. The children read materials, wrote plans, and raised and counted money. By the time the quilt was completed, many of the school's objectives for children's achievement in language arts, mathematics, social studies, and economics had been successfully met.

Another teacher of 6-year-olds rejected an invitation to attend a magic show on the grounds that her children, still in the preoperational period of thought, would not be impressed by magic. She was right. The preoperational child sees nothing magical about a bunny appearing out of a hat and disappearing again. To the young child's way of thinking, the world is full of such surprises. So the teacher substituted a trip to a nearby park to feed the ducks, a very age-appropriate choice for her group.

Knowing that 7-year-olds are interested in collecting things, another teacher pursued a number of collecting activities with her children. She provided children with scrapbooks, boxes with dividers, clear plastic containers, egg cartons, and a variety of other containers. When the Boy Scouts held a stamp show, she made plans for the children to visit. Fascinated with the idea of collecting stamps, the children explored the role of government agencies in processing mail, and the nature of the United States postal system. The children use mapping skills as they located nations on a globe, and developed art appreciation skills as they examined stamp designs from different countries and created

their own special stamp.

Eight- and 9-year-olds want to be independent. Teachers of 3rd- and 4th-graders should give their students the opportunities to make their own plans for parties, excursions into the community, and group projects. For example, a group of 3rd-graders, echoing their parents' concern about trick-or-treating, suggested that they might put on a special show for the school on Halloween and plan a party for other primary-age children. With the teacher's help, the class decided to adapt "The Twelve Days of Christmas" into the "The Thirteen Days of Halloween." The entire class worked together to rewrite each verse of the poem, compromising when their ideas conflicted.

At first, the class considered making costumes and being actors, but soon rejected the idea; they decided that they, not the parents, should be the creators of the entire production. The idea of a puppet show appealed to them. In small groups, the children took over the responsibility for creating puppet characters for each verse. They checked arts and crafts books and sought advice from art and music teachers, as well as from parents. They made modifications in their plans and used problem-solving strategies. In one instance, when they determined it was going to be too difficult and time-consuming to make 12 skeletons, the children changed a verse so that only one skeleton was mentioned. Small groups planned the lighting, scenery, and music; assigned the parts; and organized the show's rehearsal; nothing proceeded until the entire class gave its approval, however. The entire class made refreshments and invited other classes to the show.

This does not mean, of course, that every project in a developmental program is a whole-group endeavor. Individual children have their own interests, and these, too, should be respected and nurtured. One teacher noticed that two girls were constantly bringing her decaying or moldy things they had found, either in the classroom or on the play yard. In great excitement, the girls brought her a piece of bread covered with greenish mold. On another day, they spent a great deal of time playing with a can of paint that had spoiled and begun to mold.

Taking her cues from these two girls, the teacher found several books on molds for them to read. She provided them with magnifying glasses to better explore molds, and she planned a special field trip for them to visit a scientist in a laboratory. To help the girls summarize their experiences, she asked them to report to the total group and plan an exhibit on molds for the classroom. Although the other children didn't become as involved, the exhibits did attract several other children, and the girls became "experts" who responded to their classmates' curiosity and to visitors' questions.

Progressive Growth. Children's maturational interests, needs, abilities, and inabilities continually change, becoming more complex and sophisticated as they age. Because children's growth is hierarchical, meaningful curriculum will be progressive. Across the preschool and primary grades, progression is built into the curriculum when teachers "spend their time observing children, working to uncover their point of view and understandings. They use their observations to guide their plans and actions" (Curtis & Carter, 2000, p. 3).

If next year's children are as interested in leaves as this year's group is, Consuela's unit can be extended. The children might group leaves by their arrangement on trees. Do the leaves appear on the trees in alternate, opposite, linear, haphazard, parallel, or paired patterns? Perhaps they might observe leaf vein networks and categorize leaves by that characteristic. Children's questions about leaves should be encouraged and various ways of answering them explored. For example, in a 2nd-grade class where children were measuring various objects with different units, one child posed the problem of measuring the area of irregular objects such as leaves. Working in groups, children measured the perimeters of several leaves with different devices and then graphed the results.

As children study about the trees from which these leaves came, more sophisticated questions about conservation can be explored: the type of soil required by different trees, the kinds of trees growing in different parts of the world, and the ways that trees benefit the environment.

More complexity and abstraction can be added with each extension. By the time children complete the 3rd grade, even though they must still rely on their immediate environments as the primary source of data, they begin to realize that their knowledge of trees can be expanded through books and other media, and by listening to experts.

Individual Patterns of Growth. Despite the fact that all children progress through the same stages of growth, each is an individual personality with a unique pattern and timing of growth, learning style, and family background (Bredekamp & Copple, 1997). When teachers account for these different patterns of growth in their planning, they can provide meaningful curriculum.

Continuous observation of children and personal interactions with individual children permit teachers to develop an understanding of each child as a unique person. Teachers not only observe children, but also talk with them, their parents, and their former teachers, and can learn more about them through visits in their homes, communities, and former classes. Thus, they gain a greater understanding of each child's abilities, experiences, interests, developmental levels, and ways of viewing and organizing knowledge.

Many different patterns of learning behaviors and interests are manifested in any one classroom. Some classrooms have a wider range of differences than others. Children with physical challenges, children whose home language is not English, and children with learning disabilities may all be in regular classroom settings. These children's interests must be encouraged and their learning needs accommodated. In a classroom based on developmental continuity, the collaborative atmosphere, variety of experiences and activities, and small-group work support the learning of children with special learning needs (Edmiaston, 1998). Since all children do not participate in every activity, it is much easier to individualize instruction based on each individual's particular strengths. Theme-based learning, meaningful and purposeful literacy activities, and curriculum planned around children's interests are hallmarks of a developmental classroom; these approaches have been recommended as particularly supportive for children who are learning English as a second language (Perez & Torres-Guzman, 1995).

The child who is unable to stay on a task, but rather flits from activity to activity, must have encouragement and support in trying to focus for a bit longer each day. The child who gets stuck on a task and cannot let go, making little progress, may need a teacher's help to find the courage to try something new. Some children will learn new skills as they observe, try out activities, or interact with others. Other children will need more direct modeling or more structure to their instruction. To devise a curriculum that responds to individual children's needs and interests, a teacher must recognize children's preferred learning modalities (visual, auditory, kinesthetic, and/or tactile) and provide opportunities for children to use their preferred approach (Kovalik & Olsen, 1997). Teachers may find Gardner's work (1993) in the area of multiple intelligences helpful in shaping the classroom environment to offer children the chance to experience learning from many perspectives.

The key to developing a successful learning community is building relationships among the children (Dalton & Watson, 1997). Children can and do learn from each other, and teachers need to guide their experiences in working together. By carefully structuring activities that help children get to know each other early in the school year and observing children working in pairs and groups, teachers support children's developing skills in working together. A friendly classroom helps children feel comfortable and confident, and it supports the development of individual interests and abilities.

The experience of two 1st-graders helps illustrate this point. Antoinette selected Tommy to work with her on a geography project. She was learning English and found that she could ask Tommy what a word meant without being ridiculed. He always tried to explain and was patient with her when she tried out the word again and again to see if it worked in new situations. He even praised her sometimes and told Mrs. K what she had learned. Tommy benefited as well, for he developed greater skill in explanation and Antoinette's questions often led him to reflect about what something meant and how he knew it.

Some children, at times, may need to work individually on a project. Knowing when to pull back and require group work also may be necessary. No one wanted to work with Susan because she was so bossy. She was pleased to work by herself, and made great strides on her part of the "road construction project." When it came time to put the various parts together and join the others, however, she wasn't willing to compromise her ideas. The teacher met privately with Susan and concluded that Susan needed more experiences working with other children as she was not making sufficient progress toward this 3rd-grade classroom's objective of learning to work cooperatively. Susan agreed to try some group projects, but only if she were allowed to choose her partners. They reached a compromise. Susan's teacher agreed to start with a supportive partner, but said that at other times he would expect her to try working with someone he selected. Gradually, by the end of the year, Susan was better equipped to move into the 4th grade, where she would be expected to do many group projects.

KNOWLEDGE OF
THE ENVIRONMENT

"You know," Consuela continues to Claudia, "I think of curriculum as a dynamic thing. I really do base what I do on the outcomes and standards of my school system. But how the children meet these depends on their interests, their maturational needs, and their culture. Because I want children to be active learners, I also look to their neighborhood and community as I make plans."

Each community has its own characteristics, and these characteristics can add meaning to the curriculum. Simply taking a walk through the children's neighborhood(s) can give one an idea of the community's racial, socioeconomic, and cultural components. An understanding of the child comes from an understanding of the environment in which the child lives.

Lucy Sprague Mitchell (1934) explained it this way: "It is the school's job to begin with the children's own environment, whatever and wherever it may be. The complications of the surrounding culture, instead of making this attack impossible, make it imperative" (Mitchell, 1934, p. 16). The role of the teacher, she said, "is therefore to study relations in the environment into which children are born and to watch the children's behavior in their environment, to note when and how they first discover relations and what they are. On the basis of these findings, each school will make its own curriculum for small children" (p. 12).

A program based on developmental continuity understands and respects the traditions and life view of the child's community and culture. For example, a teacher on the Navajo reservation who understood something of the traditions and cultural viewpoint of children and their families did not select the topic "Bones" as a curriculum experience, although it was included in the guidelines (Ortiz & Loughlin, 1980). In the Navajo culture, talking about and handling bones are considered inappropriate.

In an effort to provide a developmentally continuous classroom environment, teachers can visit places of interest in the community to talk with the people about the services they provide. These experiences help one build a sense of the community and, at the same time, make one aware of its resources. Content from curriculum guide units or class-selected themes makes more sense to children when the resources are familiar. Beginning the lessons with materials from children's immediate environments helps them to discover and explore additional resources in their own communities.

Every community has natural resources, people resources, and material resources. Visits to the local library can reveal information about the community's special features—parks, museums, zoos, recreational areas, shopping plazas, business districts, industrial areas, churches, and transportation depots. The library also can provide details of the community's topology and ecology. Becoming better acquainted with community resources means teachers become collectors of ideas and materials. They get answers to such questions as, "What materials can I get for free from commercial establishments?," "What places in the area would be good for a field trip?," and "Which people would be useful visitors to the classroom?"

Teachers also collect information about children's experiential backgrounds. What knowledge or materials do children pick up when they play in the community? What trees, flowers, and insects are children likely to notice? Are there shop windows to look at on the way to school? Are there signs they might read? Smells to notice? Sounds besides those of traffic? Knowing about the community, with its sights, sounds, and smells, will help teachers plan a curriculum that builds on children's prior knowledge and experiences. When a teacher uses fabrics from the local shops as backgrounds for bulletin boards or as table and shelf coverings, for example, children see the colors, patterns, and textures of their cultures reflected in the classroom.

Knowledge of children's environment extends beyond the immediate "here and now." Today, children are bombarded with all types of information from television, videos, radio, magazines, movies, and from the adults who care for them and love them. In the wake of the terrorist attacks of September 11, 2001, teachers struggled to help young children cope with the horror. In classrooms where children were accustomed to using many modalities to express their ideas (Gross & Clemens, 2002), boys and girls used paint, clay, markers, dramatic play, and conversation to express their emotions and resolve some of their confusion and uncertainty during that turbulent time. Rather than banning or discouraging play or art that contains violence, teachers seeking developmental continuity in their classrooms recognize that children need opportunities to express themselves with and to people they trust.

CURRICULUM CONTENT

Meaningfulness also must extend to content. Whatever is presented to young children must have integrity in terms of content. Content is just as whole and continuous as children's growth and development. Just as children cannot be separated into segments for social, emotional, physical, or intellectual development, so content cannot be presented as separate and discrete subject matter. Themes or units of study emphasizing concepts key to a given discipline or subject matter help to unify the curriculum.

During the 1990s, professional associations and organizations responding to the push to standardize curriculum developed standards for concepts key to their respective disciplines. For example, scientists, educators, and discipline content area specialists from the International Reading Association, the National Council of Teachers of English, the National Council of Teachers of Mathematics, the National Council of Teachers of Social Studies, the Consortium of National Arts Education Associations, the National Science Foundation, and the National Association for Sports and Physical Education each identified standards in their field.

These standards describe concepts key to the specific content areas. Not only do the standards identify what the student should be able to know, understand, and do, but many also address what the teacher should do as well.

In addition, most states and local school districts have developed standards for achievement in various content areas for each grade level. These provide a continuum of learning goals and objectives in each content area, from kindergarten through the secondary grades.

These standards, however, whether developed by national associations or local institutions, generally do not provide a complete continuum of learning. Few address the preschool or early childhood years. The National Council of Teachers of Mathematics has developed standards for preschool; most, however, begin with standards for teaching and learning in the kindergarten. A number of states as well as some private organizations have addressed the preschool years by developing standards for learning. McGraw-Hill, for instance, has developed pre-kindergarten standards, which are available on its Web site.

In the past, teachers of young children had little information about what children should *learn* and *be able to do* at a given age. Teachers had a great deal of information about what children knew and could do as a result of maturation; exactly what they were to teach to young children, and what children should learn, was unclear. Child-centered teachers would claim they taught "the whole child," not separate subjects.

On the other hand, the current push for standards may have resulted in teachers having too many expectations about what children are to learn. Any one set of standards for any grade level could take up the entire school curriculum, not just for a year, but throughout the children's educational lifetime. As just one of many examples, *Geography for Life: National Geography Standards 1994* (National Council on Geographic Education, 1994) states that students should know and understand the location of the continents and oceans; understand parallels and meridians; and be able to locate major physical and human features around the world. The standards document also determines that children should be able to identify physical and human features, use mental maps, draw maps, analyze locations of places and describe why certain activities take place in these locations, as well as identify connections among places and explain the causes and consequences of spatial interactions.

Although a number of standards developed by professional organizations advocate integration with the entire curriculum, such as the *National Standards for History for Grades K-4: Expanding Children's World in Time and Space* (National Center for History in Schools, 1994), and the *National Science Education Standards* (National Committee on Science Education Standards and Assessment, 1994), and reflect the idea of developmentally appropriate practices, most do not. Thus, the standards could be used to develop a separate subject matter curriculum rather than an integrated, unified curriculum.

With this plethora of information about what content is critical to a given subject area, teachers assume the role of decision-makers. Regardless of the work of professional associations, teachers still must ask themselves, "What of this content matches the interests, needs, abilities, and strengths of the children I teach?"

Considering their knowledge of young children and their environment, coupled with knowledge of standards from all content areas, teachers must ask:

• *From this body of knowledge and subject matter, what holds meaning for this group of children, and to each individual child?* Knowledge of standards from any subject matter area develops gradually. Remember that children have a long time to grow and learn; as they do so, they will have many experiences with similar ideas and the content listed in any given set of standards. The content teachers introduce to children will depend on children's level of understanding, their interests, and teacher goals and resources. For example, preschoolers would learn concepts related to measurement as they poured sand or water from one container into a larger container. On the other hand, 2nd-graders might get involved in weighing containers and recording, on graphs, which container holds the most.

• *What aspects of this standard could be introduced to children through their own firsthand experiences in the classroom or through community field trips?* While many events in the classroom allow children to expand their knowledge of a subject, field trips and field work can extend this understanding. For a study unit on molds, children could observe molds, read about molds, and conduct simple experiments, and they also could visit a research scientist in her laboratory to find out how professionals study molds.

• *What ideas or understandings do children already have of this content?* Young children's inability to articulate, define, or describe a concept does not mean they have no knowledge or understanding of it. Children do cooperate, yet few 6- or 7-year-olds can define cooperative behavior. Six- or 7-year-olds do draw maps and can use them to find a hidden treasure at a party, but will not be able to use and understand the abstract concepts involved in true mapping, such as scale, dimension, or a key for map symbols, until age 11 or 12.

• *How can this standard or content be integrated with what children have already experienced or learned in the preschool, kindergarten, or previous grade?* Children in one school in a port city visited the harbor each year. In successive years, their teachers would ask what they remembered about the harbor and would set up specific things to investigate during the current year. By the 3rd grade, these children had investigated such things as: types of ships using the harbor, various home ports, products shipped into and out of the harbor, jobs related to the harbor, the history of the harbor, and the environmental impact of the harbor.

• *What elements of this specific concept does a novice learner need to learn now?* In other words, teachers must differentiate between what a young child knows, understands, or discovers about a subject and what the competent, proficient, or expert learner knows.

PROCESS OF PLANNING

"I really appreciate your ideas, and you've given me some very good guidelines to follow, but how do you know what do?" Claudia wonders. "And are you using the curriculum guides at all?" LaVerne chimes in.

"Well, it is a continual process of thinking and planning," Consuela responds. "I operate my classroom by establishing an overall schedule that is flexible enough so that I can reorganize the children's day, if interests and projects require extended time periods. I call these periods 'workshops.' During these workshop times, the children may be working in small groups or individually. Before and after each session, I usually plan time for total group sharing and processing of ideas. I also have a framework of the skills from the different disciplines that children should be acquiring. I've tried to become familiar with the standards that each discipline's national organization has developed. You might want to take a look at a book I found—*Curriculum in Early Childhood: A Resource Guide for Preschool and Kindergarten Teachers* (Schickedanz et al., 1997). The authors have done a great job of listing objectives that derive from the national standards in various disciplinary areas, and they include great examples of theme-based units. My district's curriculum guides also have lists of skills as well as themes and unit suggestions that I use. Beyond that, I try to be flexible enough so I can respond to children's interests and needs."

Consuela adds, "Perhaps it might help if I took you through

the process that I am going through right now to extend the children's interest in leaves to a study about trees.

"First, I've been checking the curriculum guides to see if I should be focusing on some important themes. I found that environmental issues relate greatly to a study about trees. Children are concerned about what effect events have on their lives, and the environment certainly affects them. So, an over-riding question for this study will be, 'What effect do trees have on our lives?'

"When planning, I usually try to think of some important con-cepts and skills that children would learn from such a study. I will probably begin the study by using a K-W-L chart. At the beginning, we fill in the K section (Know) with all the things the children currently know about trees. In the W section (Wonder), we begin to list questions that we would like to investigate. We'll continue adding to that section as the study unfolds. As we learn things, we fill in the L section (Learned) of the chart, and record the new information we have acquired through our study of trees. Charts are a great way to keep track of a study and document what we are learning.

"Presently, we are focusing on 'setting' in reading and on 'map-ping' in social studies. I am looking at books and checking on ma-terials to see if this study of environmental issues can be integrated into the skills the children are developing in these areas of the curriculum.

"One of my greatest sources for ideas are the wonderful children's books available. In my search I found *Are Trees Alive?* (Miller, 2002), which compares trees to people and clarifies the concept of what makes something alive. I also found one by Gail Gibbons called *Tell Me, Tree* (2002). This one identifies all the parts of the tree and provides a way to identify many com-mon trees. Since one of the children brought in a leaf from that marvelous old apple tree on the edge of the school yard, I've decided to start the study off by reading *Johnny Appleseed* (Benel

& Benel, 2001). This version is a narrative poem that tells the story through wonderfully evocative language and illustrations that the children will enjoy.

"Although we'll add new concepts and probably new skills as our themes develop, I'll describe some of the concepts, skills, and activities that I am going to begin with" (see Study of Trees, p. 67-68).

"I believe I have enough material to start this week's project," Consuela reasons. "Some of the presentations or projects will be total class, but others will require children to work in groups or individually. This weekend, as I gather the books for children to read and gather my materials to see how many groups I will have working at one time, I'll decide on group arrangements for guided reading. I'll have several book choices for the children to select from. We'll discuss what they discovered from their readings, and the children will have choices about how they wish to represent what they have learned.

"As a total group, we will discuss some of the findings and plan out the different projects: topography, time lines, creative stories, or reports. Three basic work areas will be prepared; depending upon the children's discoveries from their reading and their interests, however, children will choose whether they will be a part of one, two, or all three activities. The maps, the time lines, children's journals, and creative stories will give me information about what students have learned. At the end of most of our units of study, I ask the children to reflect on what new information or new skills they have acquired. You see, I am trying to get them to become aware of their own learning."

A curriculum of developmental continuity is carefully thought out. It is developed with the school or community expectations in mind. Children's universal stages, as well as individual patterns of growth, are accounted for. Curriculum content covers all disciplines— reading, writing, math, social studies, science, art, music, physical education, and drama. However, this content is presented as an integrated curriculum and involves children in active learning. Although children are in charge of their own learning, the teacher is responsible for the content, for developing a continuity of experiences, and for providing opportunities to use both written and oral language to express their understanding and knowledge. Classroom social interactions that are important to curriculum development are provided through shared common experiences, flexible grouping patterns, interactions with the teacher, and opportunities for children to reflect upon their learning.

Continuity of curriculum is successful when the classroom environment reflects the respective growth patterns of the preschool, kindergarten, and primary child, and when it takes into account individual differences. Children who move abruptly from a play-like, child-oriented environment to an academically and teacher-oriented environment are likely to have difficulty making sense of the content to be learned. To ensure early school success, it is important that each classroom setting be geared to children's developmental levels, and that changes in structure be introduced gradually and on a continuum.

Study of Trees

Use a small branch of the apple tree in the yard as a stimulus for connecting leaves to their trees (total group). Select a tree in the school yard as a class tree and observe it regularly for the rest of the year, taking photographs and noting changes in *science* journals. Children may also select an individual tree in the yard or community to study.

Find out what the children already know about why trees are important to us and what questions they might have about trees. Record this information on our K-W-L chart (total group).

Read *Are Trees Alive?* (Miller, 2002), *Tell Me, Tree* (Gibbons, 2002), and other books to the entire class for general discussion relating to the concepts that children can learn about trees (total group).

Some possible concepts are that trees:

- Are alive
- Can be identified by various parts: leaves, bark, shape
- Change during the seasons
- Provide joy, delight (aesthetics)
- Provide shade and shelter for insects, birds, and other creatures
- Contribute to air quality.

Using a balanced approach to literacy instruction (Avery, 1993) means time will be available in the schedule to read aloud to the children, as well as for small-group and individual reading. Already established literacy centers and other learning stations just need some modifications to reflect the current area of study. Children will have a wide variety of books on trees to select for individual or paired reading. Select these books to reflect the range of reading levels in the class; the media specialist can help organize these by ability level, so the children can select books to read that are appropriate for them. Use related stories from the reading anthology, little books, and basals for guided reading with small groups. Fountas and Pinnell (1996) have good ideas on how to proceed. Of course, books about other topics may be used.

In *reading,* children are studying the setting of the story. From reading books about trees, they can examine the setting (and, thus, the kind of environment that trees need). Concepts of setting are:

- Where does the story take place?
- When does the story take place?
- Do the time and place change throughout the story?
- Do people or things change with place or time?
- What in the book clues us in to the time and place of the story?

Add specialized words found during read aloud, guided reading, and individual reading to the word wall, so that children can use this vocabulary in their own writing about trees. Use these words for word study as well, similar to ways suggested by Pinnell and Fountas (1998).

Children will *write* regularly in journals and during writers' workshop. Encourage them to create stories, poems, and/or reports about the trees they are studying. As they are reading about trees, they will be encouraged to write responses to their books (individuals).

- What is the setting for my book?
- What things did I learn about trees from this book?
- What would I like to read more about?

In *social studies,* children are studying mapping skills (total group for developing or modeling the process of doing the activity, and small groups for completing activities). On global maps, children will locate the places where their stories take place and put identifying stickers with the title of their book on the maps. Children will make topographical maps of the school yard and community, and place models of their trees in the appropriate places. This project will involve making three-dimensional tree models (clay, cardboard cutouts, pipe cleaners for trunks, small sticks for branches, and colored paper for leaves) and for making a large map, with various topographies represented. Integrate this project with *mathematics* by working with measurements, estimation, and standardized systems, and study the trees and leaves for symmetry.

Symmetry also might come up when the children have opportunities to use art materials to represent their study of trees. Tell the school art teacher what is being studied; sometimes he or she will be able to integrate the art program with the study. Include *art* in the classroom, through a center that allows children the opportunity to be creative.

Children will also create time lines for months or years using such coding as "In my time," "When Mother was young," "When Grandpa was young," etc. Children whose books reflect the passage of time will illustrate on the time line how the trees change over time. Introduce this concept by reading children parts of the fascinating book *While a Tree Was Growing* (Bosveld, 1997), which places historic events within the life span of a redwood tree.

CHAPTER 5

CONTINUITY OF ENVIRONMENT

"I'm finding I need a new classroom arrangement and lots more materials if I'm going to have strong curriculum content, plus allow for children's development levels," states Claudia. "You two must have some suggestions for me. How do you manage, Consuela, in a 2nd-grade classroom? And Laverne, you have Head Start children. Haven't you changed classroom arrangements so that you balance the children's need for academics and social/physical involvement? Do either of you have access to floor plans?"

"Well," responds Consuela, "I had several, and I visited Laverne's as well as other preschool and primary classrooms. I even visited a Waldorf School and a Reggio Emilia-oriented school. It all helped, but the difficulty I had was that those plans didn't fit too well into my classroom setting. I tried one plan, but the outlets, bookcases, and bulletin boards didn't coincide with the recommended plans or the activities I envisioned. So, I experimented with different arrangements. Flexibility is really the key! Since I have older children, we can do some rearranging for specific projects. We do have to do some negotiating, of course, when private spaces are altered for the common good."

"It's amazing what you discover when you're willing to experiment," pipes up Laverne. "At one point I was giving in to the pressures of formal reading activities—even for 4s. Then I discovered an amazing thing. My 4-year-olds were doing more 'reading and writing' in the block area than at the reading/writing corner! It started when a few children built a rather fancy truck out of blocks. They wanted to put a sign that read Milford Fire

Truck on the side. We all went to the reading/writing area and I helped them write their sign and attach it.

"Well, you know how children are—I was overwhelmed with requests. I started to devise strategies so the children could begin to write their own signs. It was especially helpful to make word lists of things they might make and post them in the area. Their writing took off—copying some of the letters became the thing to do. Then one child discovered the title of the book he was using had the word he needed for his project. So, at least for a while, books stirred up more interest in words. Plus, by putting notepads and pencils in the housekeeping area, I found more children did pretend writing or scribbling. I feel more confident now in explaining to administrators or parents how children are learning important reading and writing skills. I'm even finding I can assess their development as they participate in center activities."

W hen teachers are able to adapt curriculum for each group of children or for individuals, there is no one way to arrange the space or materials in any given room. However, curriculum authorities believe that the arranged environment will communicate the teacher's expectations for children's learning. The arrangement can communicate to children that they are expected to be socially, physically, and intellectually active, or it can indicate they are going to be passive recipients of someone else's knowledge. It can invite children to give free rein to their intellectual curiosity, or inhibit their need to discover and learn (Leland & Kasten, 2002).

Because children under age 7 or 8 learn through activity, the physical environment can reinforce the teacher's efforts to challenge children's intellectual, physical, social, and mental activities. Classrooms arranged with centers of interest give children spaces to learn, either by themselves or within groups. These spaces will have a variety of appropriate materials, and the daily schedule will permit active learning. With appropriate goals and objectives for her group in mind, the teacher provides an arranged environment that challenges children to think, motivates them to explore, and entices them to find out the answers to their questions.

Figure 5.1

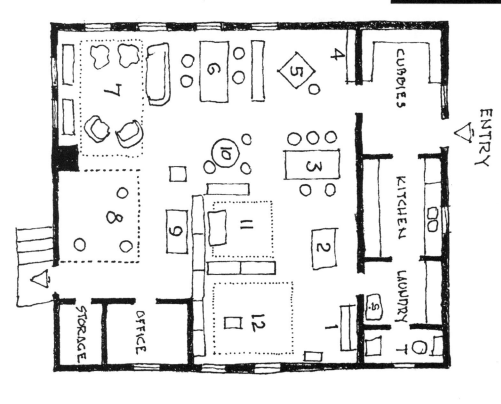

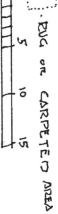

— OUTDOOR PLAY SPACE —

1 · MUSIC · PIANO
2 · WATER TABLE
3 · MESSY ART TABLE
4 · PARENT LIBRARY
5 · PAINTING EASEL
6 · ART TABLE
7 · READING AREA~ COUCH / CHAIRS
8 · LOFT~ DRAMATIC PLAY
9 · WOOD WORKING AREA
10 · CLAY TABLE
11 · PUZZLE / MANIPULATIVE AREA
12 · BLOCK AREA / TRUCKS

· RUG or CARPETED AREA

0 5 10 15

THE PHYSICAL ENVIRONMENT

Every classroom should be arranged so as to invite children's exploration of and experimentation with a variety of print, audio, and graphic resources (see Figure 5.1). In these explorations, children will ask questions and seek answers from adults, peers, or computers. In addition, children's own musings and creative energies are a rich resource for learning. The environment also should be structured in a way that fosters both oral and written expression that can be "shared" with someone else. Whether in a preschool or one of the primary grades, the classroom will have the materials and resources detailed below.

SIMILAR, YET DIFFERENT

Classrooms across the preschool and primary grades will be similar in many respects. They will also differ, however. A program that provides for developmental continuity will be one in which the spaces for children's learning, and the materials within these spaces, change to match children's continuous development. The space also must reflect a balance among skill development areas of reading/writing, math, science, social studies, and physical education—and also present opportunities for practicing, transferring, and using these skills to acquire new knowledge.

Spaces may be conceptualized on a con-

AN INVITATION TO EXPLORE

From print and other graphic materials

From a variety of audio/visual or tactile materials

From computer programs and Internet sources

With adults and with peers

With one's own inner resources

FLEXIBILITY OF WORKING SPACES FOR

Individuals in personal and private spaces

Small-group activity

Total-group activity

SPACES FOR PROJECTS/ CONTENT LEARNING

Writing	Art
Reading	Music
Science	Drama
Social Studies	Movement
Mathematics	Physical Education

AREAS

Library

(Reading/Writing/Listening centers, with a variety of books, print materials, writing implements, paper, cut-out and magnetic letters, word lists, small chalk or wipe boards, tape recorders and tapes, computer set-up)

Creative Arts

(painting, drawing, modeling, writing, designing)

Crafts and Construction

(construction blocks, sand table, water table, creations)

Dramatic arts

(housekeeping/office/etc., stage area, costumes/props, puppetry, flannel board)

Music/Movement

(musical instruments, record players, tape recorder, scarves, and other props)

Manipulatives & Math

(puzzles, games, patterns, sewing, measuring, cooking, real cameras)

Physical Activity

(balls, bats, jump ropes, bean bags, mazes, hopscotch chalk)

FURNITURE

Tables	Chairs
Bookcases	Shelves
Filing cabinets	Rugs

STORAGE AREAS

(Kept orderly and interesting to children)

For children's belongings

(easily accessible for children)

For the teacher's materials

For those materials that children need permission or assistance to use

tinuum from the simple to the complex, from adult-supervised to child-supervised, from concrete to abstract, and from those requiring few skills to those using refined, complicated skills. Space will balance children's need for academic learning with their growing need for socialization, emotional maturity, and physical development (Pangrazi, 2000).

Spaces Become Increasingly Complex. Classrooms designed for developmental continuity recognize children's growing cognitive, physical, and social skills. Therefore, materials in the centers, the ways the spaces are used, and flexibility and use of time become more complex throughout the preschool and the primary grades.

For example, the art center should include implements for painting, drawing, and collage experiences; through center activities, the children should move from experimenting with the different materials to gaining control over the materials, and even exploring another artist's vision of a theme or subject. In one classroom, a child drew what he called a robin, inspiring other children to become interested in birds. As time went on, the teacher introduced photos of some birds and discussed various aspects of bird life. Picture books of artists' interpretations of bird movements became models for the children's work. The displays of their work, which the children had titled, allowed them to compare their use of media. Such experiences not only extend children's art exploration but also connect children to reading and writing experiences (Zimmerman & Zimmerman, 2000).

Movement activity is another example of more complex use of space; expanded space plus added materials (such as scarves and a variety of rhythmic instruments) will be required. Young children need both indoor and outdoor space for experimenting as they refine their large motor skills by moving in different directions or interpreting stories through hopping, jumping, and running. Later, children learn to refine movements, to move to different rhythms or patterns, and to interpret stories or even their own "reports." One group of children used movement to communicate with their class information about their pretzel-making experiment. They tried out various movements until they were satisfied that they could communicate all the steps: adding and stirring the various ingredients, watching the dough rise, twisting the dough into shape, and finally baking the pretzels in the oven.

As teachers and children use space in more complex ways, they discover how music, art, drama, and movement allow children to demonstrate their increasing understanding of reading, math, science, and social studies concepts, as well as their ability to work together and solve problems (Smith, 2002).

Spaces Gradually Require More Responsibility. A program based on developmental continuity is one in which children will learn to use space wisely, productively, and responsibly. They will be expected to use spaces with increasing independence, such as in their work centers. Three- and 4-year-olds are expected to be responsible for selecting the center they will work in each day. Kindergarten children have the added responsibility of caring for the materials in the centers. By the 3rd grade, with limited adult supervision, children should be completely responsible for helping to prepare and restock materials for the centers, caring for them, and working independently.

Preschool children will need adult help in getting ready to do easel painting and to clean up. In the 1st grade, children can be expected to mix their own paints. By the 2nd grade, they can mix paints to create new colors and use a color shell to identify complementary colors. At this point, children can prepare paint sets placed in containers, enabling them to take the paints to another room, the hallways, or the play yard when they need more space for their projects.

Spaces Move From Concrete to Abstract. In environments that are responsive to children's cognitive development, the classroom spaces and materials become increasingly abstract across the preschool and primary grades. Young children learn by handling concrete materials. At first, these materials are simple and reflect the children's reality. The preschool classroom, for example, can provide big blocks and realistic materials related to the children's immediate environment, so that the children can build constructions and enact roles relating to their everyday experiences.

Consider how children's block play gradually moves from concrete, specific use to more representational use. In kindergarten, large blocks and unit blocks extend children's cognitive development. Since children now understand that objects can have more than one use, materials from other parts of the classroom are linked to the construction areas. For example: writing materials from the writing center can be used for making signs to name constructions, empty food boxes from the housekeeping area could serve as grocery items in a make-believe grocery store, blankets from the doll's bed can serve as a curtain for a newly designed stage, and chairs from the center of the room might serve as seats for the audience.

Very young children develop literacy skills as they interact with more concrete materials; older children may continue to use concrete materials as a domain for developing more abstract concepts and greater literacy skills (Nels, 2000). Primary classrooms should provide materials that are useful for multiple purposes. A range of informational books and writing materials added to the different areas will encourage children to solve problems and create new designs as they construct projects, write stories, or paint pictures. All types of ordinary household materials become functional in a classroom committed to children's experimentation and level of maturity. For example, cotton can be used to represent the bunny's tail on a painting, or clouds on a diorama, or fog at the seashore in a sand construction. Popsicle sticks can serve as a base for a puppet, as building materials for a small fort, or as a marker on a sand hill to indicate the distance a ball rolled.

Spaces and Materials Demand Ever-Greater Skills. The spaces and materials provided ought to reflect the children's growing physical and intellectual dexterity. Even within a classroom, spaces and materials must allow for variations. The construction areas in classrooms for younger children will be different from the ones provided for older children. Older children can work together with less supervision, so a larger table should be provided to accommodate team projects. These construction areas give children opportunities to pursue practical applications of math and measurement skills, as well as opportunities to be creative.

In a classroom for 3- and 4-year-olds, children are given instruction and practice on using one tool at a time, with the teacher closely supervising those having difficulty. In kindergarten, experienced children can choose to construct an object that requires both hammering and sawing. By 1st grade, children can follow directions for working on a construction that requires measuring, sawing, hammering, and gluing. By 3rd grade, children who have had these previous experiences can design and then create their own constructions at the woodworking table.

In classrooms for children ages 5 to 7 or 8, not all of the materials need to be available to all children at all times. Certain spaces and materials that are appropriate for a given age or skill level may be rotated for use at different times of the day, or on different days. As projects develop, certain areas may be set aside for one particular group of children.

ARRANGING SPACES

"Where should I put the library area?" "Do you have a floor plan I can use?" There is no one way to answer these questions, because there is no one right way to plan spaces for developmental continuity. Nor is there any particular formula for selecting and arranging equipment and materials within spaces. To start, however, it is helpful to think of dividing the classroom into four large areas: a large movement/ rug area, an area for desks or tables and chairs, a reading/writing area, and a construction/math science area. Then, each teacher makes decisions about how to accommodate projects and learning activities, based on knowledge of children's growth and development, an understanding of each individual child, societal expectations, and his/ her own comfort level (Seefeldt & Barbour, 2001).

Flexibility of space is also vital, because teachers will create more meaningful curriculum as they note and respond to children's questions and ideas about their natural world (Hughes, 2002). This thought process can begin by asking the questions "How can the available spaces best be arranged to reflect what I now know, and yet allow for change as I learn more about my class?" and "What space considerations apply to any special needs of the children?"

Reality of Physical Space. Teachers need to realize that some aspects of the classroom are not subject to change. A teacher cannot change the size of the room, nor the windows' and doors' locations. Within the space given, however, teachers can arrange furniture and materials so that they maximize flexibility for children's social, physical, and cognitive activities, and allow for ways to expand the available space.

One teacher began by drawing a floor plan of the classroom and sketching in the electrical outlets, a sink with running water, access to the corridors and the outdoors, storage spaces, and built-in shelves (see Figure 5.2). She then asked herself what kind of furniture was available, and which items could be traded for furniture that could be used more flexibly. She found some tables and small desks that were easily moved and could be rearranged and regrouped for different projects. Using her drawn plan and looking about the room, she asked herself:

What safety features will need to be considered? What is the lighting? What kind of wall space is available? Can work or materials be suspended from the ceiling on pulley-like arrangements, without affecting the lighting or the pleasantness of the spaces?

Next, teachers plan ways to *expand* the space through the use of hallway spaces, other rooms within the building, and outdoor spaces. Because learning is not confined to the classroom, the spaces and learning opportunities within the community also are considered. When considering these extra spaces, however, it is also important to consider how these spaces are to be supervised. Will you have dependable volunteers or aides? Are the spaces close enough so that responsible children can use them with minimum supervision?

Consider whether the corridors can be used for group work. Will fire and safety codes be violated? Will other classes be disturbed? How will the flow of traffic be affected? If hall spaces can be used, can these areas be used at all times, or just at specific times? Can the work be supervised? Will children be responsible enough to work independently? How will you be able to supervise them?

Other rooms and spaces in the building usually can be found. The media center, the gym, or the cafeteria can be used occasionally for special projects, for appropriate individual projects, or for total group endeavors. Rules and regulations will need to be established with the children so that productive use of the space is made. The teacher will need to determine if any school rules and regulations govern use of such spaces.

When planning to use outdoor spaces, ask: Is the space accessible only through a common door to the building, or is an exit to outdoor space available in the classroom? Is an outdoor space available next to the classroom that would be used only by that class? Is it paved? Is it grassy? Could art, water and

Figure 5.2

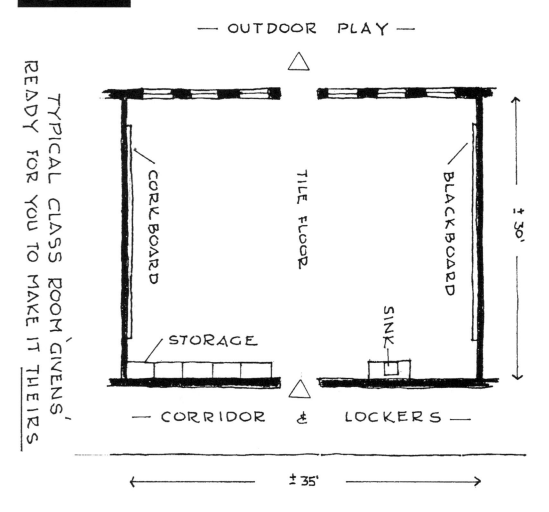

sand, and/or certain types of building or experimental projects be pursued safely, with minimal supervision? If the outdoor space available is a communal space, what limitations apply to its use by an individual class?

At some point in the planning process, the teacher also needs to consider the space in the larger community: the learning opportunities for the children to be found within a short walk of the school; places where a small group of children—with an aide or volunteer parent—can go to collect data for a project (with adequate community support, individual children might be able to pursue a project in the community); business enterprises that can assist in expanding children's understanding of their environment and natural environments (Rivkin, 1995).

Also consider display opportunities. Do any of the outside-the-classroom spaces provide opportunities for display of children's work? Can the corridor walls be used? Are display cases or spaces where projects can be set up available? Would any local stores or businesses agree to display children's work? (Some public television stations and public libraries will do so, as will some shopping centers.) What criteria should be established for each of the display areas? What varied opportunities can be found that allow each child to display what he/she does best, or that challenge a child to strive for improvement?

Reality of Who the Children Are. As teachers plan how to arrange the spaces available to them, they need to consider the children's characteristics. This may be difficult, for children change during summer vacation, and different children may be enrolled in the school. Still, some considerations can be considered ahead of time.

Often, the cultural diversity and the socioeconomic diversity of prospective children is known and teachers can make sensible adjustments. In some cultures, for example, children are expected to share everything, and so they may have little sense of privacy. In others, children are encouraged to share, but their culture emphasizes privacy and a sense of personal space. Based on a knowledge of their students' different cultural perspectives, teachers can decide whether they will need to provide more communal space or more personal space to accommodate children's differences. Those children who are accustomed to sharing and have little or no experiences with personal ownership will need space that permits them to learn, share, and work together while learning to respect those children who feel possessive about their own space and materials. The latter children will need to feel that they have personal space before they will be able to share and work with groups.

The age, maturity, physical development, range of developmental levels, special needs, and possible interests of the children may be known if they are returning students. Check to see if desks, tables, and chairs of varying sizes are needed to accommodate children of different heights. Consider arranging the space so that children who need to move around even while working can do so without disturbing those who need more private space for concentrating.

Children's previous experiences may be determined from school records, or may be discovered from the character of the surrounding community. Special arrangements are needed to accommodate children's special needs, interests, and talents. For example, live animals can enhance children's learning, but some children may be allergic to furry animals; by setting aside space for aquariums or terrariums these children can explore fish or plant life. Some children can be responsible for petting, feeding, and caring for pets that can live in cages. Children who are especially interested in artistic pursuits will need more space and different art media. Children with hearing or vision impairments will need special seating arrangements and a careful layout of pathways. Carefully consider how you could accommodate children's talents with special space arrangements.

Howard Gardner (1999) maintains that different intelligences exist that "form their own distinctive form of mental representation" (p. 72), a view endorsed by those educators who believe that children have different learning styles. Most authorities now acknowledge that different spaces are necessary to accommodate learning through these various intelligences. By observing other ways of acquiring knowledge and providing different spaces, teachers can ensure that children's learning is enriched. For example, to develop their linguistic abilities, children need spaces to read, write, tell stories, and do word puzzles. For logical-mathematical development, spaces are needed to compute, do experiments, and play strategy games. To develop spatial intelligence, children require space to engage in building, creating pictures and images, and designing or "inventing" things. All children benefit from having space to develop musical ability, which means particular spaces are needed where they can listen to music, play instruments, sing songs, and move rhythmically.

Space is needed in which children can move, touch various objects, and act out their ideas as their bodily-kinesthetic intelligence develops. Spaces need to be provided that allow them to use their large muscles in jumping, running, and climbing; woodworking, carving, and sewing activities will hone their fine motor skills. To acquire interpersonal abilities, children need several areas in the classroom where they can work and socialize in groups. All children will enhance their learning as they develop their abilities to work independently, and as they learn to develop their inner resources and intrapersonal skills (Gardner, 1983).

In his later work, Gardner (1999) also identifies naturalistic and existentialist intelligences. While all children learn from the natural environment, some seem to be more attuned to this sphere than others, suggesting they may have a "naturalistic" aptitude. Classroom pets and plants, cloud formations, ant hills, and geologic formations are more intriguing to some children than to others. They need time and space to observe and discover things about the natural world.

Although young children usually do not examine deep questions about the meaning of life and about their observations of the natural environment, many children will puzzle over what makes clouds form such different shapes or why the ants swarm when some sand is dumped on their hill. They will question why they lost a beloved grandparent. Some believe in a magical power that allows the traffic light to change or the rain to stop so they can play. These musings might be considered precursors to an existentialist intelligence. Gardner (1999) posits that when educators introduce important concepts that respond to the different ways children learn and think, then more students will succeed in developing their observation skills. And all children will learn how to tap into inner resources for greater enjoyment and understanding. By providing spaces for different learning styles and respecting children's differences, the teacher encourages all children to experiment and expand their ways of knowing.

Reality of Societal Expectations. Often, schools or parents have expectations that must be taken into account when planning for space. Both parents and taxpayers are right to expect that children in any classroom will show growth and progress toward achieving reading, writing, and mathematical skills. Each year, children should gain new knowledge about the world around them, as they develop problem-solving and creative skills. Children also should show progress in developing physical powers, as well as their interpersonal and intrapersonal skills.

Teachers also should consider specific types of expectations for the children in their classrooms. For example, do parents expect phonics and number facts to be learned as precursors to reading and problem solving? What specific science or social studies content is deemed important? What are expectations regarding the role of art, music, and movement/physical development in children's lives? What aspects of the children's various cultures are expected to be reinforced? Bowman (1989) suggests that when culturally based differences exist between home and school expectations, these discrepancies must be confronted directly. Thoughtful teachers can help children make meaningful connections between their experiences and the new context of schooling.

Space arrangement and use of appropriate materials will help communicate to visiting parents that efforts are being made to boost children's development in key areas of the curriculum. Children can elaborate on their previous experiences in their writings, projects, reading, problem solving, and experiments. These learning projects should be a part of the classroom decor, and the space where these events occur should be evident.

Reality of Goals and Objectives. Teachers' goals and objectives vary from school to school and classroom to classroom. In a classroom organized around continuity of experiences for children the teacher's aim must be to nurture growth and learning so that every child remains curious and eager to learn. Children will acquire specific skills, attitudes, and knowledge at different rates as they progress through school.

To plan the use of space so that children will be able to achieve certain goals, the teacher should ask the following questions:

- Will children show growth in their problem-solving ability? In their comprehension of a variety of printed matter? In their ability to express themselves orally, artistically, musically, and in writing?
- Will children's understanding of and interest in the natural world about them be expanded? Will the children become more independent in their work habits and skill development? Are the children becoming more skilled at working with a group to accomplish a task, and are they better able to function in a large group? Are they becoming more physically adept and secure in their own abilities?

Reality of the Teacher's Own Comfort Level. Teachers have strengths and limitations that affect how they will plan the physical environment. Some questions they might ask include:

- Is there an easy flow of movement so that I can tolerate the noise level?

- Are spaces for noisier activities far enough away from quiet activities so that children can concentrate?
- How can I arrange the room so I will not find it necessary to reprimand children for their more active involvement?
- Do children have easy access to materials without needing help in getting the materials or in putting them away?
- Are areas arranged so that appropriate materials may be stored nearby?
- Are some spaces flexible enough that different numbers of children with varying interests can work there, without too much need for rearranging?
- Are areas arranged so that I can supervise all the projects, but still have space for assisting individual children or small groups?
- Is the space arranged so that I can feel in charge, without having to feel that I must control all the activities?
- Will materials be handy for my use, as well as for the children's?
- Do I need personal space in the classroom, and will I have some?
- Will I have an aide or volunteers to assist in the classroom? Do space arrangements accommodate the extra adult(s)?

A CASE STUDY: ARRANGING THE PHYSICAL ENVIRONMENT

"You can examine several different plans, or better still, visit in different developmentally appropriate classrooms, Claudia," explains Consuela. "But perhaps it would help if I share some of the thinking I did as I organized for my 2nd-grade classroom. You know, in some ways this was a good challenge. It did force me to think much more about how to arrange the space so that children's different developmental levels would be taken into account.

"The *first reality* I had to confront was that the *space in the classroom* I was assigned was much too small for all the activities and projects that I envisioned (see Figure 5.3). One of the walls had a bank of windows. Although I love all the light streaming into the room, I could clearly see there wouldn't be sufficient space to display all of the children's work. The first thing I did was to check out ways to expand the space. Two things were in my favor. First, the classroom is at the end of the corridor, so a minimum of traffic went by. Second, I have an outside door that leads directly onto a courtyard.

"The *second reality* that I confronted was the *maturity of the children.* Could they deal with the *third reality—my expectations and those of the school?* I was correct in my assumption that many of the more mature kids could assist the younger and less mature students in staying on task. By establishing with the children expectations for their behavior, both inside and outside the classroom, and by being consistent regarding those expectations, I eventually succeeded in using other spaces. I initially experimented with using the hall for individual projects or for occasional small-group work. I scheduled larger groups only occasionally—when I knew I would be able to check on them more often. This year, because I am more comfortable with how to use out-of-classroom space, I suspect I will find more opportunities to function safely in the corridor, outdoors, and other places in the school.

"I have always had a number of different ethnic groups in my classes. It is both a *school goal and parental expectation* that children share their cultural events in various ways, especially during some of the major holiday seasons. The extra outdoor and corridor space became important as we set up long tables for the Passover Seder and a paper dragon for the Chinese New Year.

"Last year, knowing that I would be able to find additional space, I made several sketches for my actual classroom space, noting important fixtures, outlets, shelves, etc. I divided the classroom sketches into four unequal quadrants, allowing for *flexible spacing*

Figure 5.3

POSSIBLE SPACE ARRANGEMENTS   - DIVIDED BY LOW SHELF UNITS
USE COMBINATIONS OF THESE TO CREATE SPACES BEST SUITED TO YOUR CHILDREN

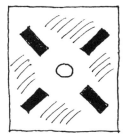 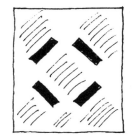 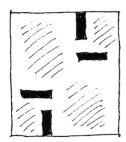

for small-group, total-group, and individual activities. I tried to consider how children could have some personal space, as well. The extra sketches enabled me to try more than one scheme. Fortunately, shelving is available on three sides of the room, so the activities that I planned did include space for easily accessible materials.

"One of the larger areas contained children's desks (see Figure 5.4) clustered in groups of six. Such an arrangement not only saved space, but also allowed for total-group instruction as well as small-group activities. While the desks were used for children's 'private space,' I could also rearrange them at times to provide for small-group work and for individual projects. At first, some children were highly incensed when others used 'their' space, but we worked it out, since the private lockers outside the classroom are indeed 'private.'

"A low bookcase with shelves on both sides separated the desks from the second large space. Writing materials, different types of paper, and books of different reading levels, organized in baskets, were placed on shelves facing the desks. There also was space for children to leave their current journals or portfolios at the end of the day. At the beginning of the day, children collected their work folders and their journals and kept them in their desks. Materials to take home were kept in their lockers. Special books for leisure reading and informational books were placed on the shelves on the other side of the bookcase. A rug placed between the bookcase and the chalkboard created a 'meeting space' for total-group instruction or discussion. The space was big enough for children to sit in a circle, although at times we used more unstructured sitting arrangements. For example, I like to read a story to all the children at the end of the day, allowing some of them to stretch out gave a more relaxed and enjoyable atmosphere to the reading experience.

"Nearby chairs allowed those who needed to sit away from others to do so while remaining part of the large group. During other times, the meeting space often was used by two, possibly three, small groups. Placing a bookcase near the rug invited children to select books and read and browse in a relaxed manner on the rug, or to share the book with a companion.

"The third and fourth areas of the classroom contained the activity centers. These area centers will be quite different this year, and this is my thinking about the rearrangement. First, I'm putting a sand table and water table nearer the sink. The art table and the construction area will be near the windows. Since children demonstrate their knowledge of topics studied through concrete objects, as well as through writing, these areas provide rich resources.

"Built-in shelves in front of the bank of windows have a wide ledge on which I will display children's three-dimensional constructions. The shelves beneath provide places to put art and construction supplies, books related to the projects, and even extra writing materials and math manipulatives and games. I found last year that by having writing/reading materials easily accessible in the activity areas, the children tended to extend their story/journal writing and their use of books to check out some of their ideas.

"The outside door in the center of the bank of windows and

OUTDOOR PLAY

Figure 5.4

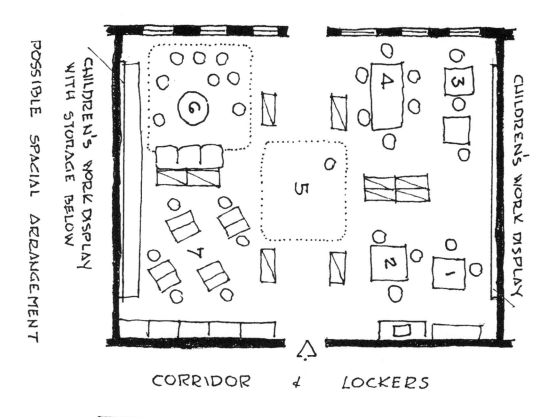

POSSIBLE SPACIAL ARRANGEMENT

CHILDREN'S WORK DISPLAY WITH STORAGE BELOW

CHILDREN'S WORK DISPLAY

CORRIDOR & LOCKERS

1. WATER TABLE
2. SAND TABLE
3. WOOD WORKING
4. ART
5. MULTIPURPOSE-GROUP PLAY
6. READING + STORY TELLING
7. INDIVIDUAL DESK SPACE

□ . LOW SHELF UNITS

⬭ . RUG

ALL UNITS MOVEABLE

the entrance door separates the more active areas from centers requiring quiet concentration. The multipurpose group play area is in the center of the room. Bookcases or desks separate this area from the rest of the classroom. The CD/tape recorder, music and story tapes, and CDs are stored in the reading area, but I find that the children often take the portable tape recorder to various areas. They listen quietly in the reading/story telling area, or they find a more private desk space. They also play music for movement activities in the center space when blocks aren't being used there for construction activities. Using the blocks, some children even constructed a sort of 'theater.' One child got his 'group' to arrange chairs around the rug, and he invited the rest of the class to see a performance.

"Last year, as I arranged the furniture to meet my requirements, I walked around the room, checking the ease of movement and envisioning the flow of traffic. I moved to different places in the room to make sure I could observe and supervise the children from wherever I might be. This step was a wise one, for I did find a few problems that I solved before school began. This was an important step.

"After making these major decisions, I reviewed the framework to determine if all major considerations were met. There were obvious spaces for writing, reading, mathematics, and art, and for some social studies/science projects. This year, I will try to make my science projects more evident at the sand table, with additional water activities, and the new woodworking bench. By examining the framework, I realized I hadn't been as careful with music, drama, and movement. With the concern for overweight children, I want to be sure that I can get children to be more actively involved, even while teaching them more academic content. I am working with some very enthusiastic parents, and we are planning some music and drama activities that will not only help children move, but also enhance our reading and writing activities. Having the two rug areas should really help.

"Puppetry, flannel boards, and prop boxes for drama are stored in the closet. Children reenact stories from their reading and report their project results in a type of performance at one of the rug areas. Last year, as they used the prop boxes, we improvised adding other costumes and prop boxes. For more formal events, and as the children gain independence, I can allow children outdoor space to practice their performances. Different projects suggest which prop boxes, flannel board material, or puppets are needed. I know from last year's experience that the children and I will be able to create new prop boxes for this year.

"Musical instruments, and additional records and tapes, also are stored in the closet. Again, the rug areas are good spaces for learning and practicing songs, and for restricted musical movements. For large movement activities, we used the outdoor space. A music teacher (and room) is available to assist with music endeavors; some children, of course, have private music lessons.

"Cooking, while quite common in my classroom, was always a planned activity. The shelf beside the sink served to hold the small oven and portable burners, and some things were taken to the cafeteria for baking. It worked well last year. The cafeteria staff was very responsive and we worked hard to maintain their trust. Several tables in the classroom were used for mixing and preparing of foods. Last year, it was exciting when one of the cafeteria workers had a small group help her in the kitchen to prepare a special treat for visiting parents.

"Wall space in the classroom for display work is always a bit of a problem, especially since I am anxious to demonstrate to parents what the children are learning. Certainly, I found last year that I needed more space to display children's work, as well as for displays that invited children to explore, informed them of procedures, or answered some of their questions. Of course, the large chalkboard in front of the room and a large bulletin board in the back of the room were both handy, especially for ever-changing 'exhibits.' This year, I will use the closet doors near the desks for posting project directions, and the entrance door for posting notes from children to their parents. Children initiated this endeavor at the end of last year, and it was a HUGE success.

"One part of the bulletin board was used for display of children's papers, and on another section we displayed group discoveries. The tops of the shelves were reserved for three-dimensional projects. Last year, the children got the idea of suspending some projects from the ceiling, but it really didn't work too well. This year, I will be placing a bulletin board outside the room for special displays. As the year progressed, a part of the chalkboard in front of the rug area was designated for children's daily messages to each other, or for certain safety messages. That also was the children's suggestion, and it worked very well.

"The arrangement for my classroom provided children with freedom of movement and materials for exploring—similar to classrooms using a project approach. This arrangement helped the children to develop more maturity and independence—important considerations when using a less well-supervised space. As the year progressed, the children became much better at working cooperatively and were more willing to help each other learn. The children worked together many times, even on complex projects.

"We all learned to respect each other's work. Less mature children were often challenged, but all the children did realize that they learned many different things from each other. It was most evident, probably, when children shared their unique experiences. For example, one child had visited a volcano site in Hawaii. Another group of students were collaborating on a story that included a volcanic eruption, but were struggling with the setting description. Imagine everyone's delight when

Bobby became the class 'expert.'

"Although I'll make some changes this year, even after the children arrive, this initial planning will provide a good beginning. The space allows enough freedom of movement for children to explore, investigate, or ask questions of adults or peers, but it is restricted enough that children learn to cooperate and not be overly intrusive of those who need to work independently."

SOCIAL/EMOTIONAL ENVIRONMENTS

The physical environment supports children's social/emotional and intellectual development. Teachers also use space to provide the necessary emotional support for their children.

Brain research reinforces Piaget's theory that children are constructors of their own knowledge. In order for children to become competent, their developing brain requires a supportive and nurturing environment for social interactions and intellectual pursuits (Shore, 1997). If classrooms are to provide environments that foster pursuit of knowledge, then the social/emotional climate must foster both security and challenge. As children mature, greater challenges must be made available.

With the appropriate physical arrangement, atmosphere, and social interactions, classrooms can encourage children to explore, experiment, and solve problems. Or these classrooms can intimidate, discourage testing of one's abilities, and limit questioning.

Physical Arrangements

Whether a room is arranged for a preschool child or a primary-age child, the organization of space either permits freedom or restricts movement. Rooms organized for exploration should have several open space areas that allow for a natural flow of activity, with boundaries restricting movement for safety reasons. Although boundaries may suggest different types of activities to be carried on in each area, experimentation requires that space be flexible and that areas have the potential of extending beyond rigid boundaries.

Younger children need more open space as they move about the classroom. Although they are learning the fundamental movements of running, jumping, skipping, hopping, and leaping, they do not have such movements under control. Older children still need space for large muscle movements, but they have more control over these movements and should be learning to move adroitly within varying amounts of space.

Children understand what their environment permits them to do from the types of materials available and the ways they are organized. When materials can be used in more than one way, children know that their unique visions of how to structure their learning will be accepted. Materials that must be used in only one way can frustrate children who haven't the interest in or skill for that purpose, or they can bore children who have mastered their use.

The amount of materials in a classroom also can foster or hinder healthy social development. Young children generally can attend to only one or two material features at a time; too many choices of materials or activities can overstimulate or frustrate. Likewise, too few materials can be problematic. Young children have difficulty sharing or waiting for a turn; therefore, insufficient materials can lead to fighting, squabbling, or relying on a teacher to monitor the activity. For older children who are learning to cooperate, having only one of each kind of tool in the classroom can force them to figure out how to reach a compromise.

CLASSROOM ATMOSPHERE

Anyone works better in an atmosphere where individuals are respected, have choices, and encounter expectations that are not beyond their abilities. In addition, preschool/primary children work best in a climate that allows them to be active learners. They will show their enthusiasm for learning as they move about the classroom and talk to their friends and adults about many things.

Young children are exuberant and often quite noisy. Their talk can be loud as they shout across the room to a friend, and they can be annoying as they interrupt peers and adults out of an impatience to share. Unrestricted movement and talk do not show respect for others. For this reason, children need to learn, in a supportive atmosphere, how to be active without intruding on another's activity and how to share ideas without always being first.

In a classroom where action is prized and children are expected to explore, conflicts will arise. Young children are egocentric; only gradually during their primary years do they begin to understand how someone else feels or that the other person may have a different point of view. As children develop, they need to feel secure in expressing their feelings. When children do not have the verbal skills to indicate their frustrations or anger, they resort to physical reactions. Teachers who provide a positive classroom environment devise strategies and use classroom events to help children express their own feelings and understand how someone else might feel.

Having children talk things out, modeling appropriate language to use, and role-playing feelings are three useful strategies. Careful observation and knowledge of children can help teachers support children's growth.

Three-year-old Tian usually showed her displeasure by hitting her companion. Tian's teacher was encouraging her to use words instead to express her feelings. At first, Tian's behavior did not seem to change much. Then came a breakthrough. One day while playing with her friend Joe, Joe accidentally hit Tian's head. Tian looked very startled; Joe looked ready to cry. Fearing retaliation was about to happen, Mrs. T, an alert teacher, moved to the area and said, "Tian, I think Joe is very sorry. I don't think he meant to hurt you." Tian then said. "When you hit, it hurts!" "Yes, Tian, it hurts," Mrs. T replied. Tian then turned to Mrs. T and asked, "If *I* hit *you*, it hurts?" Mrs. T responded, "Why yes, Tian, when you hit anyone, it hurts." "Even Joe, or my baby?" "Yes, Tian, Joe or your baby." During the day, Tian periodically would ask about hitting other people and how it hurt, as if this were new information to her. Tian's behavior began to change. A positive environment, where she could learn how her actions affected others without fear of rejection, gave Tian the support she needed as she began to realize the consequences of her actions.

SOCIAL INTERACTIONS

Young children are egocentric and other-directed. It is through interactions with their peers that they successfully develop the ability to perceive another's point of view and become autonomous or self-directed.

Whatever the age of the children, rules for classroom behaviors must be established. Younger children will respond to the rules simply because an authority figure has established them. They may forget the rule, however, if it prevents them from doing what they wish. Tian knew that she was not supposed to hit, but she continued to do it whenever she didn't get her way. The teacher remained patient with her and used Tian's own experience of being hurt to help her change. Even 3s and 4s can begin to formulate a few simple classroom rules themselves and remind each other when rules are violated.

During the primary years, children take rules literally and begin to accept responsibility for their actions. They are becoming self-directed. When conflicts arise because of different behavior patterns, children can be supported in learning to solve these problems and formulate their own codes of behaviors. Freeing children in this way not only results in more positive behavior, but also leads children to take responsibility for bringing up and resolving the conflicts. One group of 2nd-graders was distressed because too much sand from the sandbox was getting on the floor. In a meeting of the entire class, the students raised the issue, brainstormed solutions, experimented with some of them, and then reformulated the rules. Primary children do not always come up with sensible solutions, nor can all solutions be tried. Children need guidance in selecting those that are plausible and recognizing which are out of bounds. A secure emotional environment that frees children to express even absurd ideas without being ridiculed gradually teaches them how to focus on more reasonable ones. They learn these skills through experimentation.

Talk is necessary for social interactions. Teachers who insist on quiet classrooms all day long do not provide the opportunity for children to explore how others feel and think. Some teachers believe that children should be free to talk only if they remain on task. A great deal of children's talk while they are engaged in activities, however, is not what one would call "on task." Yet, this talk can help children get along with others, resolve conflicts, or make discoveries.

One group of 3rd-grade children was conducting an experiment at the water table, testing ways to make their homemade sailboats move faster. They were asked to give a report to the total group at the end of the morning. Josh began to use one of the boats like an airplane. Sandy, a more task-oriented child, became frustrated and went to "tell the teacher." Instead of intervening, the teacher suggested that Sandy needed to resolve the conflict with Josh herself. Upon returning to the group, Sandy asked Josh how they were going to report on which boat went faster if he didn't stop fooling around. Josh figured they couldn't. He put the boat down, saying, "You guys can finish this; I'll find something to explain how it works," and he went to get a book. The rest of the team members finished their "tests" and were ready for the report. Josh contributed by informing the class of the hydroplane boats and the speeds that they could reach—information he gleaned from his reading. He and another child became interested in figuring out how to replicate other boats besides sailboats. Later, others in the class designed different boats and tried to figure out how to give their homemade boats more power.

A classroom where social interactions are encouraged, and where children have the freedom to make choices about their activities, provides for much richer learning experiences. The children's social/emotional development supports their more academic and intellectual pursuits.

INTELLECTUAL ENVIRONMENT

An intellectual environment in any classroom ensures that all children, as well as the teacher, are learning. Skilled teachers re-create the curriculum with the children as they initiate units and themes that require children to develop math, reading, writing, and social studies/science skills. They also build on children's interests while appealing to their curiosity.

Materials invite exploration and offer choices. The competent classroom has a variety of materials that can be used in simple or complex ways. A few materials may have a single use, but most materials can be used in many different centers and for many different purposes.

As children are encouraged to experiment, teachers likewise feel comfortable in experimenting. They observe the children, reflect on what is happening, pose questions, and evaluate their growth. Teachers who provide an intellectual environment also model curiosity and a desire to learn more. They experiment with ideas, testing to see if different materials or conflicting information will challenge the children's thinking. As they rejoice in children's learning, teachers share their own enthusiasm for new skills or new information they have acquired.

Children from preschool through primary grades require an environment that takes into account their growing independence. The physical, social/emotional, and intellectual environments of all classrooms, regardless of the children's ages, should allow for explo-

ration. As teachers arrange space, they take into account the realities of their situations: the actual classroom dimensions; the age, maturity, and culture of the children; the goals and expectations of the school and community; and both the teacher's and the children's comfort levels.

Knowing that classroom arrangements have flexible working spaces, appropriate furniture, and adequate storage and display areas frees the teacher to plan for content areas, using a wide variety of academic, constructive, and creative materials. The social/emotional and intellectual climates provide the security and challenge that invite children to explore and learn.

CHAPTER 6

CONTINUITY OF ASSESSMENT

"What a hideous week!" exclaims Claudia. "We have been doing standardized testing, and I feel that all the work I've done to change instruction in my class is being negated. Consuela, what do you do when you and the children are being evaluated on measures that seem contrary to the goal of meeting children's individual needs?"

"It's so frustrating!" agrees Consuela. "High-stakes testing is getting out of hand all over the United States. And when academic progress is measured by a single test and major decisions—like if a child can be promoted or not—are attached to the test, then rich, high-level teaching and learning get sacrificed to test preparation. I was reading an article in *Childhood Education* (Terzian, 2002) that describes how schools in Chicago can get 're-engineered' if their standardized test scores don't improve. All the teaching and administrative staff get dismissed and new ones are hired. They haven't done anything like that in my district, but there has been some talk about our salary increases being related to increases in children's achievement on the tests."

"So how do you cope with the pressure of these tests?" persists Claudia.

"Well," responds Consuela, "my children are improving their skills in math, reading, and writing through my developmental curriculum. I am constantly informing parents and administrators about how the children are progressing. I am all for assessment! I want to be accountable for what I have been helping the children learn. But I feel very worried about the way standardized tests are being used with young children.

Many national organizations have taken strong stands in regard to standardized testing of young children—the Association for Childhood Education International (ACEI) (ACEI/ Perrone, 1991), the National Association for the Education of Young Children (NAEYC) (1988), and the National Association of State Boards of Education (NASBE) (1988). I've been trying to read as much as I can about standardized testing so that I can speak out against what I have come to see as a real threat against quality teaching and learning. I liked Ohanian's (2001) article on that very idea."

"What have you learned?" Claudia asks.

"Well," Consuela replies, "for one thing, American children are being tested more now than ever before and more than anywhere else in the world. It also seems that this is a political issue—it's the politicians and business community who are pushing for more testing, while those in the education community are expressing reservations. One thing that really got to me—Laverne, you're probably well aware of this from working in Head Start—is how test scores correlate so highly with family income and other socioeconomic factors, such as parents' jobs, level of education, and the stability of the neighborhood. Many educators believe that rather than measuring what is learned in school, standardized tests reflect what children have learned outside of school (e.g., Wesson, 2001). And children with limited English proficiency are at a real disadvantage when it comes to the tests that require reading. Even if the students understand the math, they stumble on the word problems. And as we all know, young children don't develop the same skills at the same time, so expecting them all to have acquired certain knowledge by testing time is unrealistic and unfair. Even when children do know something, they can't always express their knowledge in the way called for on the standardized test format. We all have experienced the emotional fall-out that some children experience during and after testing—crying, acting stressed, feelings of failure. I could go on and on about how standardized testing puts undue pressure not only on children, but also on teachers. The teachers feel that they must prepare kids for the test and thus adopt a curriculum that is not the most effective kind of instruction."

"Well, don't you do anything to help your children get ready for the tests?" wonders Laverne.

"I do, but I try to do the least amount while focusing on helping my children feel confident and capable of doing what is needed. Alfie Kohn (2001) is a strong advocate for eliminating testing with young children, and he suggests that a short, intensive test preparation period is more helpful than a curriculum keyed to the test. Kohn has written a lot in this area, and he contends that increased testing actually lowers standards (2000).

"So I try to do what Thompson (2001) suggested—I balance helping my children do all right on the tests my district requires, while working toward changing the policy relating to testing children. The 'Work Sampling System' of Harrington, Meisels, McMahon, Dichtelmiller, and Jablon (1997) is one approach that has been developed as an alternative to the use of standardized tests. If we don't believe in standardized testing," continues Consuela, "we have to keep working on an effective assessment system to show that it isn't that we don't want to evaluate children, we just want to do it in a way that doesn't harm them and that shows what they really do know."

"I can see that. Laverne and I have been discussing our mutual need for better ways of assessing children and reporting their progress to parents," admits Claudia. "It does take time to correct all those papers I give them and to record the results; all the testing we do really takes a lot of time. But it seems to me that observations, checklists, interviews, and portfolios will take even longer, and that I won't have time for the many things we are beginning to do in our classrooms."

"Any assessment system takes time," concedes Consuela,

"but the hardest part is determining an approach to classroom assessment, developing an organizational system, and then communicating to parents and administrations accurate information about each child's growth and learning. I had to experiment with different ideas before I found what was comfortable for me and for the parents. Now the kindergarten and 1st-grade teachers use similar strategies, and we find we have so much information to share with parents during the fall and spring conferences. I'll share with you what we are doing."

"A DETERMINING AN APPROACH TO ASSESSMENT

t our school, we developed an approach to assessment that involves a number of strategies to collect information about individual children," says Consuela. "Each is a form of authentic assessment as described by Montgomery (2001), because each is related to the curriculum and the ongoing activities of the classroom. The basis of our approach to assessment is observation. We determined that what really helps us to understand how children are developing is to listen to children, observe them in action, and document what we learn in the form of anecdotal records, interviews, and checklists. We collect these observations, as well as samples of children's work and teacher-constructed tests, in individual portfolios. An important part of the portfolio is the child's self-assessment of particular work samples and overall progress."

OBSERVATIONS

Teacher observation of children engaged in classroom activities is the foundation for an authentic approach to assessment. The benefits to children's learning yielded by observation is bolstered by a growing body of literature, much of it written by teachers themselves (e.g., Gallas, 1994; Paley, 1984, 1988, 1990; Pelo & Davidson, 2000). Teachers of very young children have always found observation to be a necessary aspect of assessment. Now, teachers in the primary grades are increasingly discovering its importance. Even though teachers may observe informally all of the time, and may spontaneously record children's activities, amusing statements, and even behaviors that are cause for concern, Cohen, Stern, and Balaban (1997) make a strong case for a more formal approach to observation and recording. Curtis and Carter (2000) present an approach that accounts for allowing the teacher to shift her observation of individual children over the course of the year. In the beginning of the year, a teacher may look for information about:

- How a child behaves during routines and transitions
- How a child uses the classroom environment and materials
- How a child gets along with other children and adults
- The child's use of self-help skills
- The child's use of language.

As the year goes on, teachers will expand their observations to determine:

- How a child solves problems
- What skills the child may need to experience greater success
- The child's developing language and literacy
- The child's engagement in math, science, art, music, and all other activities of the school.

While many ways to successfully observe children's behavior in the classroom exist, it is crucial that all observations be recorded. Written records preserve details that can be amplified later, using various strategies that teachers can adapt to their own styles and circumstances (Nilsen, 1997). Many teachers have found it useful to carry a small notebook or note cards in their pockets or on a key hook attached to their belts. Others use a clipboard covered with Post-it notes that are labeled with the name of each child they are planning to observe. During the day, teachers periodically make brief notes about their observations of specific children. To ensure that all children are observed, each day they pick different children as the focus of their observations.

In order to use these observations effectively and efficiently, the teachers schedule a half hour each day to expand their notes into brief anecdotes about the children they have observed. They put the observation into a context, describing the child's behavior, when it happened, any pertinent antecedent events,

what the child said, the reactions of other children or adults, and how the incident ended. These anecdotes, often written on cards, then are filed under the child's name in a card file or folder. They serve as useful reminders and evidence of children's development.

"This card file is an important source of information for me," says Consuela. "This is the file I go to several times a year before parent conferences or report card time. I take the time to organize my records about each child, noting any patterns of development or learning, content or skills each child has mastered or is trying to master, and difficulties, and then I write a progress report. It is time well spent, since the parents really appreciate how well I know their children and find the documentation of progress over time to be informative."

CHECKLISTS

"Since our report cards are keyed to the performance standards and specific skills children need to be developing," explains Consuela, "I use my report cards as the basis of a checklist of 'skills to be worked on' for the children in my classroom. Each year, after observing each new class of children for about one or two weeks, I begin to tailor my checklist to the particular needs of each year's class. I organize the skills by such things as self-help skills, math skills, reading skills, social skills, and physical skills. I list the skills across the top of the paper and the children's names down the side. With the help of the computer, I can easily make personalized checklists for each skill. If I find that I am not observing certain skills, I then develop some centers that will require the children to demonstrate these skills. When I observe a child performing the skill, I record the date of the observation in the space besides the child's name and make one or two abbreviated notes to remind me of any appropriate data regarding the circumstances."

Another strategy that some teachers have found helpful is to generate a set of cards, with each child having a card. As children are working on projects, the teacher notes on a particular child's card what he/she is doing and the date. Periodically, they will transfer this information to a checklist of skills to be accomplished. This checklist gives quick information to the teacher about which children or skills have and have not been observed. Reviewing these lists helps the teacher prepare activities that will allow the children to demonstrate the level of skill they have achieved in that area.

Individual and group projects, as well as center-based activities, such as writing a brochure, making a map, creating and/or following a recipe, developing a poster, play, or book, and any number of other authentic tasks (Montgomery, 2001), can provide children with opportunities to use required skills. Checklists of skills then can be used to assess their progress. As the children engage in their activities, the teacher observes how they are using the skills, and which they find difficult, and quickly note this information on their cards and/or on the checklist of skills.

INTERVIEWS

Interviews provide another way for teachers to elicit information about what a child knows or thinks. Like Piaget, who developed his theories on young children as a result of the extensive interviews he conducted with his own and other children, teachers can use interviews to learn about children's development and growing understandings. Interviews can range from an informal conversation to a structured format of specific questions.

Many interviews take place spontaneously as the teacher and children work and talk together. The teacher asks informal questions about children's ongoing activities, such as: Why did you put that there? What will happen if . . . ? How many more do you need? These open-ended questions elicit conversation and generate information about a child's thought processes. While not especially con-ducive to conversation, teachers also can ask closed-ended questions to determine children's knowledge of specific information such as attributes, locations, cause-effect, etc. (Nilsen, 1997). By recording interviews, a teacher can create a picture of children's progress in achieving various skills.

More structured interviews also may be useful. Asking children a set of questions before and after a study of a particular topic can yield a great deal of information about children's learning. Helen Darrow (1964) suggested that teachers ask children such questions as: What can you tell me about . . . ? What can you draw or write about . . . ? What can you do to show us about . . . ? Tell all you know about nouns. What do you know about nouns? Show me a noun.

When interviewing children, teachers have the opportunity to probe children's responses by asking additional questions: Why did you say that? How did you get that answer? What might happen if . . . ? When analyzing interviews, teachers can consider the consistency of children's responses, patterns, and logic; the consistency of their errors; and the accuracy and completeness of responses.

After a project on water, 3rd-grade students were asked, "What can you tell me about the water study?" If the student was hesitant, the teacher posed additional questions, such as, "What went well for you?" or "What did you enjoy the most?" These questions, along with those seeking concrete examples of specific learnings and opinions, yielded information that helped the teacher evaluate the children's understandings and progress related to the project (Montgomery, 2001).

A combination of interviews and drawing tasks was used in one school to probe children's understandings after completing a project. Teachers pasted a sun on each child's paper and asked them to draw themselves and their shadow in relation to the sun. Before and after their study of fire safety, kindergarten children were asked to draw what they would do in specific fire situations, and then answered questions about their pictures. Using the information gathered from these drawings and statements, teachers were able to assess not only children's growth, but also the usefulness of some activities.

WORK SAMPLES

Observations, checklists, and interviews provide useful sources of information about children's progress, their strengths and weaknesses, and the concepts or skills they have not yet mastered and those they have. A collection of children's work over time is another excellent way of illustrating children's progress.

In many classrooms, children have individual folders for math, reading, writing, science, social studies, and other curriculum areas. These folders hold work in progress as well as completed assignments. Some of the completed assignments have been evaluated with a *rubric* that the teacher designed and shared with the children when they began the task. A rubric is defined as "an assessment device that uses clearly specified evaluation criteria and proficiency levels that measure student achievement of those criteria" (Montgomery, 2001, p. 56). Rubrics can assess products, process, and/or progress. They clearly show children how their work will be judged, and they encourage the teacher to clarify performance criteria and to make objective assessments.

Periodically, completed work samples are selected from the folders and put into the child's portfolio, which is a specialized collection of materials used for assessment purposes. The items from the folders, as well as photos of larger projects, duplicated pages from journals, and other materials, are selected to illustrate the child's accomplishments in meeting standards. Typically, the child and teacher would choose which items to include; the material is dated and the child and/or teacher records something about when, how, and under what conditions the work was completed, and why it has been included in the portfolio. In addition to these samples of children's work, the portfolio can also include growth charts, photos of children completing skills, and tape recordings of their speech and/or reading.

A kindergarten teacher, Regine, combined her teaching of "key words" into an assessment tool. As children became interested in words and stories, Regine would ask them to share words with her that they wanted to learn. As they did so, she asked them about letters and their sounds, the meaning of the word, and its importance to them. She then had them select what they wanted to do with their word. For each child, Regine made a separate sheet on which she kept a record of each word, the letters the children recognized, what they knew about the word, and how they used the word. She dated each entry.

In addition, as part of her reading/writing program, Regine had children dictate stories about their pictures, and she encouraged them to write. Some children used scribbles, some used mock letters, and others used letters and numbers written in a string. A few could even write their favorite words. At given intervals, Regine copied and dated samples of these stories and placed them in their portfolios. From these sources, as well as her observation records, she prepared specific information (in October, January, and May) about each child's beginning awareness of letter/sound relationships and word meaning, and their language development.

Mary, a 2nd-grade teacher, collected information in a slightly different manner. Her children were not only writing stories, but also beginning to learn to rewrite edited stories for "publication." Three times a year, Mary collected one story from each child that included the first draft, edited rewrite(s), the final copy, and the rubric. Through conferences and less formal meetings, Mary felt quite confident in sharing with parents or administrators her assessment of each child's growth in the process of writing.

Self-Assessment

Because it is important to encourage children to think about what they are doing and to reflect on their own learning, teachers have developed strategies for involving children in assessment of their own progress. Self-assessment helps children reflect on and monitor their thinking and learning.

Teachers may occasionally provide checklists, rating scales, rubrics, or other forms for children to complete as they assess their work. For materials that are to be included in the portfolio, children will provide a short narrative to describe why they have selected a particular work sample and what this work shows about their progress. Daily assessment, however, will be informal, as children spontaneously discuss what went well, what things they would change (and how), what they'll want to repeat during the next project, and what they will not want to do again.

After completing a study of different land masses, a 3rd-grade class discussed what they had learned. The conversation revealed that they had acquired important concepts, and also had learned important interaction skills:

Pete: "No one knew what a peninsula was when we began, did we?"

(Several overlapping responses of "I didn't" and "Nuh, uh," and general head shaking.)

Pete: "Well, I know. It is surrounded by water."

Jane: "An *island* is surrounded by water."

Tom: "Yeah, Pete, an island is surrounded by water. A peninsula . . ."

Pete: "Well, it has water around it . . ."

Lisa: "What does *surrounded* mean?"

(Silence for a moment. Then, Jake picks up a block and placing it in the center for all to see.)

Jake: "It means that there would be water here, here, here, and here." (His hands move around each side of the block.)

Jane grabs the block from Jake and pushing it to the wall)

Jane: "That was an *island*. Now it's a peninsula, 'cause there'd be water here, here, and here—the land is here."

Teacher: "If an island is surrounded by water, then how would you describe a peninsula?"

Tom: "I started to say a peninsula has water on three sides."

Pete: "And an island has water on four sides."

Susan: "I couldn't say or spell the word *pen-in-su-la*. I first said it like 'Pensula,' cause it reminded me of 'Pennsylvania,' but Ms. J, you helped me see the 'in' in the word. Sometimes you have to look at all the parts of a word to figure it out. I can say it and spell it 'p-e-n-i-n-s-u-l-a.' "

Teacher: "Good, you remembered that, Susan!"

During this discussion, the children shared what each one had learned, as well as what the entire group learned. They were reflecting on and evaluating their own progress.

More self-assessments take place as teachers ask children to describe their progress in specific curriculum areas. Questions can be asked about literature: What story did you like best, and why? Or about art: Which materials do you enjoy painting with? Teachers also may pose questions that call for more general evaluation of the learning process: What did you learn today? What is your best subject? What subjects do you have the most difficulty with? Why? How do you think you can learn to do that? How many things do you know now that you didn't know at the beginning of the year? How many more things do you want to learn before the end of the year?

In one 3rd-grade classroom, children kept cards about the books they were reading. Some of the children listed those books they read at home, as well. At various times they wrote different information on the card—the characters (list major/minor ones, describe your favorite/least favorite one), setting (does it change?), story events, and feelings about the book. By using their cards, the teacher could see at a glance what books (and what level, type, number) the children were reading and how they were interpreting the story. After completing social studies and science units, Richard, a 1st-grade teacher, made lists with the children of the concepts they felt they had learned. He posted these lists and at different times asked children to write in their journals what they remembered about a certain topic, as well as any skills they felt they had improved on. The lists served both to jog the children's memories and to aid them in spelling difficult words. Richard used the children's responses in their journal entries to plan follow-up lessons and as references for parent conferences.

These self-evaluations did not tell everything about the classes or individual children's learning, but they did give insights into the agreement between the goals of the program and children's expectations. Children also take more ownership of their own learning when they have a voice in assessing their progress.

"My children are so used to reflecting on and assessing their own learning," concludes Consuela, "that it's just a natural part of our work. Children keep their stories in a folder and periodically compare a new story with one they had written at the beginning of the year. They use our rubric to assess their friendly letters to make sure they have included all the parts. They graph the errors they made on their spelling tests and on the 'quick checks' of number fact knowledge. In their journals, they reflect about how much better they are at sawing, sewing, climbing the rope ladder, or hitting the ball. They keep cards on the books they have read, reorganizing the cards into various categories, such as: those I liked and those I didn't like, types of books, books with impressive characters,

or by authors. They periodically share with me how they feel about their progress, as one did who was still finding reading a struggle: 'I still can't read as good as Joey, but I did finish two stories that he recommended without any help from anybody this week.' "

TESTING

And there are tests. Teacher-constructed tests, especially those related to skill development, can provide very useful assessment and evaluation information to children, administrators, and parents. When children keep track of their own progress, even spelling and number fact tests can be motivators for additional practice.

One 2nd-grade teacher had a spelling test each week, giving both a pre- and posttest. He started off by using rhyming words or words with similar vowel combinations, adding exceptions to rules as children progressed. Children sometimes made up the lists of words they wanted "to know how to spell this week." As their writing progressed, Mr. D began to use misspelled words from their stories. Children kept their own records of achievement by developing a graph of their *improvement* scores from pretest to posttest. Since the graph named the particular spelling test, Mr. D was able to not only note children's progress in spelling but also discover what combinations of letter sounds were giving them problems.

With timed number fact tests, children can be taking the test that best supports and challenges their achievement levels. Teachers can have a series of number fact tests, all with the same number of problems. Each week, with teacher guidance, the children can select the timed test to take. In their math folder, they can keep a graph of the number of problems they correctly answered, so they can measure their own progress. As children develop skill in solving math and other types of problems, tests of various problems can be made. Children can take these tests under varying conditions, such as untimed, timed, solved on one's own, and solved with a partner. Keeping track of problem-solving progress helps children, as well as the teacher, understand how they best approach this learning.

Standardized achievement tests are not recommended for all children before the 3rd grade. These types of tests, however, may have a place for some children in a program of developmental continuity. Fundamental to any educational program is the need to assess some children's progress and achievement in relationship to other children, and to assess the program's effectiveness in relation to local or national norms. Norm-referenced achievement tests can do this. This information, in addition to the information collected in the classroom, can give insights for extending the curriculum.

To determine if children in the school are progressing in reasonable ways towards national goals, a random selection of students from one's school can be used. This information can be helpful for reassessing the school's goals.

Nevertheless, achievement tests, regardless of their type, only give one piece of information about a given child—how that child stands in relation to the norming group. Many teachers find that this information isn't very useful in planning and implementing curriculum that responds to each child's level, and they continue to rely on samples of work, their observations, interviews, and checklists to help them meet each child's developmental needs.

DEVELOPING A
PORTFOLIO SYSTEM

The portfolio has emerged as the most useful way of organizing the wide array of information gathered about children in a program of developmental continuity. Long in use by artists, who utilize portfolios to collect and demonstrate their best work, an education portfolio shares a similar purpose. Portfolios help keep track of children's progress through a meaningful collection of children's work,

anecdotal observations, checklists, recorded interviews, photographs, and other documentation collected from parents, children, school administrators, and peers. Portfolios can be collected in large notebooks with divided sections devoted to different categories, in individual file boxes, or in folders stored in large folios.

Anecdotal records can be collected in one section of the portfolio and then periodically reviewed and summarized in a narrative. This process can help focus educators' future observations of the child, and the narratives often can be used as part of the report card process. Teachers will decide to include checklists and interview records in this section, or in sections specific to their content.

Teachers also make decisions about which work samples will be included in the portfolio, and about how to categorize and judge the work. Children participate by helping with the selection process and writing reflective comments about why particular pieces of work demonstrate their skills and abilities. Some teachers follow a regular schedule in sampling work; others are more informal. Most try to include samples of work from each part of the curriculum and balance work that is teacher-initiated with work that is child-initiated. Some teachers have separate sections for child-selected and teacher-selected work.

Besides serving as an ideal file for organizing assessment data, the portfolio also functions as a communication tool. Materials in the portfolio are shared with parents during parent/teacher conferences. Filled with evidence of the child's progress in various aspects of the curriculum, the portfolio gives parents a good overview of how learning occurs in the classroom. As parents and teachers review the "evidence," parents are encouraged to participate in the process by adding significant photographs, samples of work the child has done at home, or their own observational anecdotes that demonstrate their child's growth in learning during the year. They also can write responses to materials that the teacher and child have included.

Another function of the portfolio is to communicate to individual children their progress and their importance to their teachers and parents. Children recognize that only adults who really care for them would take the time to collect these important milestones in their life. Portfolios also have been used for parent/teacher/child conferences. In one school, four teams met in a classroom at one time. The child and the parent discussed the child's portfolio, with the child explaining the work that was included and discussing his or her progress. The teacher circulated from one team of parent and child to the other, adding her comments and discussing the children's progress with the parents.

The fact that a portfolio can travel with the child to the next grade or teacher is one of its most important features. "In fact," says Consuela, "now that we're in touch with several child care centers, we are encouraging the preschool teachers there to use portfolios to record each child's progress. We call that portfolio Volume I. In kindergarten, the teacher compiles Volume II. At the end of this year, children will have Volume III. Portfolios are an excellent way of documenting children's progress over time."

COMMUNICATING TO OTHERS

"I know the kindergarten children are happy," said one principal, "but how in the world can I know what they're learning? I observe their 'published writings,' listen to children read a favorite story, and share in the final projects for many children in the school, but I need to have more specific information about what the children are learning." When teachers assume the task of changing the way educators traditionally have evaluated children's achievement and progress, they also must be responsible for communicating what their new methods of evaluation mean and how they can be interpreted. One 1st-grade teacher involved her

principal in her parent conferences. These conferences, which were based heavily on the use of organized materials in the children's portfolios, enabled the principal to see and understand the value of nontraditional methods of evaluating children.

Reporting children's progress in the conference format works particularly well, but teachers also will need to develop written reporting systems that capture the richness of children's learning in their developmental curriculum. For example, a group of pre-kindergarten teachers in the Calvert County, Maryland, school district redesigned the report card so that it better reflected their changed curriculum. Some districts have moved to a narrative reporting system, while others have aligned their report cards with the standards they have set for the children.

Curriculum, assessment, and reporting systems should reflect a unified approach that is clearly communicated to parents. This communication can begin at the first open house or back to school night, as teachers describe their programs, take parents on a tour of their classrooms, and explain how the children will spend their days in school. A letter sent to children's homes at the end of the summer describing the exciting learning that awaits is another good way to help parents understand a developmental approach. Weekly newsletters also keep parents involved, and informed about the curriculum. Once parents understand the curriculum, the assessment system makes much more sense to them. Parents also greatly appreciate occasional phone calls and notes that communicate a child's latest accomplishment.

Consuela agrees that communication is the key to establishing productive relationships with parents. She notes, "Parents love this approach to assessment. They enjoy their child's portfolio that has samples of progress in all the areas, and many often look through their child's folders, journals, or card files from which materials have been selected. So many have said to me that this is much more

MIDDLE GEORGIA TECHNICAL COLLEGE LIBRARY

useful and revealing than the report cards. It is interesting that after a while, fewer and fewer parents are interested in comparing their child with others. They start to focus on the progress their child has made. I even find that many of those 'hard to reach' parents enjoy conferences. Since the focus is on progress, they usually leave feeling proud of their children."

Portfolios of children's progress facilitate communications with children's former teachers and with those who will be instructing them the next year. If children are to have instruction that allows them to progress in a developmentally appropriate fashion from the preschool through the primary grades, then teachers of these different ages will need to discuss children's progress in very concrete terms. Examples of children's work and observations of their activities collected over several years in notebooks, portfolios, and on card files can be a starting point for discussing developmentally appropriate practices in joint training sessions or staff meetings at the beginning and end of each school year. It is important that teachers, parents, and administrators work together to ensure continuity of learning for every child.

"As I get better at observing, making quick notes, and recording, I find that the time spent each day on assessment makes it easy for me to communicate with parents at any time, and preparing for conferences and report cards takes much less time than before," notes Consuela. "I also find that many of my assessment techniques are also teaching strategies. For example, the children are really learning how to graph, since I have them graph their math skills tests and their spelling tests. Having children write about the concepts that they learned from 'the fastest boat experiment' was a teaching strategy, but it also turned out to be a wonderful assessment technique. Not only did I find out what individual children gained, but I was able to evaluate the unit as well. Besides, it is much more fun, and I learn much more about individual children, their interests, and their learning styles."

TOWARDS THE FUTURE

"This year has been an exciting one for me," reveals Claudia, when she, Laverne, and Consuela meet for their end-of-the-year dinner. "I wish I could tell you that 'developmental continuity' had been accomplished in my classroom and in my school, but I can't. I *have* learned a lot about children, about myself, about parents, and about the community where I teach, because of the changes we've been making to seek continuity of experiences for our students."

"I did tell you in the beginning that developing strategies whereby all children meet with success in a continuous and developmentally appropriate manner is not accomplished overnight," replies Consuela. "I think what is important is how you feel about the progress you have made in ensuring success for children in your classroom."

"In many ways I feel really positive," adds Claudia. "Working with Laverne, gaining support from my principal, and seeing many more parents becoming positively involved with their children's learning all means a lot. We don't have a school management team functioning as I would like, however. We're also meeting resistance from some of the other teachers who are worried that our kids won't be ready for the standardized tests given at their grade level. They can't see that we are meeting the curriculum standards, even though our organization and structure is different from what they do. I'm afraid that next year, they will turn off some of the children who are just beginning to develop reading and writing skills, because they will be focusing on preparing the children for testing."

"I'm worried about the same thing!" exclaims Consuela. "The national movement toward high-stakes, test-based reform has me worried. I am all for high standards, but the focus on tests is really narrowing the curriculum."

"I feel it, too," adds Laverne. "The pressure is really on us Head Start teachers to help our children develop literacy. I'm all for that, of course, but some of the training we have received seems to equate literacy with phonemic awareness, alphabet recognition, and phonics. Those are important skills, but they're not enough to help children become excited about learning to read and write. In fact, some of the approaches to phonics really turn young children off."

Claudia adds, "I'm worried, too. Just when I've learned that I can make some important changes in my classroom and work with preschool, kindergarten, and other primary teachers, and with parents, to make developmental continuity more of a reality for all children, a new superintendent has been hired. I've heard he is going to institute a universal kindergarten curriculum in our district that will require us to follow a prescribed approach to reading. I've made changes in my curriculum and classroom organization, and I've seen the positive results for so many children. Although I haven't reached all the children, I am anxious to learn what I can do to help them achieve their potential. I'm afraid that I will lose the authority to make these important changes. I want everyone on board for these changes, and that takes lots of time and energy."

"Yes, it does," responds Consuela. "Even though teachers have tried the ideas and strategies related to developmental continuity before, it is more important than ever to be advocates for the children we teach. We mustn't get discouraged about the challenges ahead. We must continue trying to build support from the entire community. What we are trying to do is so important. We're working to provide an environment where youngsters will be able 'to use their minds well, so they may be prepared for responsible citizenship, further learning, and productive employment in our modern economy' " (U.S. Department of Education, 1991, p. 3).

I ndeed, as Consuela notes, the ideas and strategies for developmental continuity have been successfully implemented over the years by good teachers in many schools. Unfortunately, forces within society have either supported or negated the efforts of these excellent teachers. In many school systems, parents and community service agencies have worked with teachers to provide appropriate learning environments for some children.

"Leave no child behind" is a noble sentiment that guides current efforts to reach all children. In the United States, not enough children are receiving the kind of support they need to meet the challenges that they will face in an ever-changing and more complex society. The nation has moved from an industrialized society that needed workers for the assembly line to an information society that needs workers who can use their intelligence to solve problems, and who can be flexible and adapt to change.

In the past, teachers were entrusted with educating the nation's children. Over time, however, that responsibility has been taken away. Decisions about curriculum have been made by administrators, supervisors, and legislators. Too often, this policy has resulted in a set curriculum. Some believe that if all teachers followed the same guidelines, then all children would therefore acquire the same knowledge and skills. Too many children have not learned the skills and knowledge necessary for continuous growth, however, and rigid curriculum has frustrated and impeded others. It is time for educators, parents, legislators, and business people to join forces in a concerted effort to ensure the success of all children, using the accumulated knowledge about how different children learn, and to provide schools and homes with the resources they need.

To be sure, progress is achieved with each attempt to build developmental continuity in children's early educational experiences across the preschool and primary grades. Opportunities to build on this progress still exist. More and more schools, recognizing that children do not magically change as they move from the preschool to the kindergarten and primary grades, are finding ways to build bridges between children's early educational experiences. Behavioristic, lock-step curriculum has not been successful in the past; it has, in fact, been damaging. Parents, teachers, school board members, and national leaders must continue to search for more efficient and effective methods for early education.

It is time to recognize that although children progress through similar stages of development as they move across the preschool and primary grades, this development is not equal or identical. It is time to recognize that children learn best when they are allowed to construct knowledge and that schools—whether child care centers, preschools, or public schools—must provide educational experiences that will support children's growth, development, and different modes of learning. It is time to question the overuse of standardized tests in schools and to develop more appropriate ways to assess children's knowledge. Those who are concerned about children's education, especially teachers, parents, and community support groups, must come to the forefront of efforts to reorganize schools for developmental continuity.

REFERENCES

Administration for Children, Youth and Families. (1988). *Easing the transition: From preschool to kindergarten. A guide for early childhood teachers and administrators.* Washington, DC: Administration for Children, Youth and Families and the U.S. Department of Health and Human Services.

Association for Childhood Education International/Perrone, V. (1991). On standardized testing. A position paper. *Childhood Education, 67,* 131-143.

Avery, C. (1993). *And with a light touch: Learning about reading, writing, and teaching with first graders.* Portsmouth, NH: Heinemann.

Barbour, C., & Barbour, N. H. (2001). *Families, schools, and communities: Building partnerships for educating children* (2nd ed.). Upper Saddle River, NJ: Merrill/Prentice Hall.

Beatty, B. (1989). Child gardening: The teaching of young children in America. In D. Warren (Ed.), *American teachers* (pp. 65-98). New York: Macmillan.

Benel, R., & Benel, S. V. (2001). *Johnny Appleseed.* New York: Margaret K McElderry Books.

Bellis, M. (1999). Look before you loop. *Young Children, 54*(3), 70-73.

Bersani, C., & Jarjoura, D. (2002). Developing a sense of "we" in parent/teacher relationships. In V. Fu, A. J. Stremmel, & L. T. Hill (Eds.), *Teaching and learning: Collaborative exploration of the Reggio Emilia approach.* Upper Saddle River, NJ: Merrill/Prentice-Hall.

Bondy, E., & Ketts, S. (2001). "Like being at the breakfast table": The power of classroom morning meeting. *Childhood Education, 77,* 144-149.

Bosveld, J. (1997). *While a tree was growing.* New York: American Museum of Natural History.

Bowman, B. (1989). Educating language-minority children: Challenges and opportunities. *Phi Delta Kappan, 71,* 118-121.

Brandt, R. S. (1989). On parents and schools: A conversation with Joyce Epstein. *Educational Leadership, 47*(2), 24-27.

Bredekamp, S., & Copple, C. (1997). *Developmentally appropriate practice in early childhood programs* (Rev. ed.). Washington, DC: National Association for the Education of Young Children.

Bronfenbrenner, U. (1979). *The ecology of human development: Experiments by nature and design.* Cambridge, MA: Harvard University Press.

Bruer, J. T. (1998). Brain science: Brain fiction. *Educational Leadership, 56*(3), 8-18.

Carlsson-Paige, N., & Levin, D. E. (1990). *Who's calling the shots? How to respond effectively to children's fascination with war play and war toys.* New York: New Society.

Carlsson-Paige, N., & Levin, D. E. (1995). Can teachers resolve the war-play dilemma? *Young Children, 50*(5), 62-63.

Cazden, C. B. (1986). Classroom discourse. In M. E. Wittrock (Ed.), *Handbook of research on teaching* (3rd ed., pp. 432-464). New York: Macmillan.

Chase, P., & Doan, J. (1994). *Full circle: A new look at multiage education.* Portsmouth, NH: Heinemann.

Chase, P., & Doan, J. (1996*). Choosing to learn: Ownership and responsibility in a primary multiage classroom.* Portsmouth, NH: Heinemann.

Cohen, D. H., Stern, V., & Balaban, N. (1997). *Observing and recording the behavior of young children* (4th ed.). New York: Teachers College Press.

Comer, J. P., Ben-Avie, M., Haynes, N., & Joyner, E. T. (Eds.). (1999). *Child by child: The Comer process for change in education.* New York: Teachers College Press.

Cook, L., Gumperz, J., & Gumperz, B. (1982). Communicative competence in educational perspective. In L. C. Wilkenson (Ed.), *Communication in classrooms*. New York: Academic Press.

Curtis, D., & Carter, M. (2000). *The art of awareness: How observation can transform your teaching*. St. Paul, MN: Redleaf Press.

Dalton, J., & Watson, M. (1997). *Among friends: Classrooms where caring and learning prevail*. Oakland, CA: Developmental Studies Center.

Darling-Hammond, L. (1994). *Professional development schools: Schools for developing a profession*. New York: Teachers College Press.

Darrow, H. (1964). *Research: Children's concepts*. Olney, MD: Association for Childhood Education International.

Dewey, J. (1944). *Democracy and education*. New York: The Free Press.

Dyson, A. H. (1987). The value of time off tasks: Young children's spontaneous talk and deliberate text. *Harvard Educational Review, 57*, 534-564.

Edmiaston, R. (1998). Projects in inclusive early childhood classrooms. In J. H. Helm (Ed.), *The project approach catalog 2* (pp. 1:19-1:22). Champaign, IL: ERIC Clearinghouse on Elementary and Early Childhood Education.

Flanders, N. A. (1970). *Analyzing teacher behavior*. Reading, MA: Addison Wesley.

Fountas, I., & Pinnell, G. S. (1996). *Guided reading: Good first teaching for all children*. Portsmouth, NH: Heinemann.

Galen, H. (1991). Increasing parent involvement in elementary school: The nitty-gritty of one successful program. *Young Children, 46*(2), 18-28.

Gallas, K. (1994). *The languages of learning: How children talk, write, dance, draw, and sing their understanding of the world*. New York: Teachers College Press.

Gardner, H. (1983). *Frames of mind: The theory of multiple intelligences*. New York: Basic Books.

Gardner, H. (1993). *Multiple intelligences: The theory in practice*. New York: Basic Books.

Gardner, H. (1999). *The disciplined mind: What all students should understand*. New York: Simon & Schuster.

Gaustad, J. (1998). Implementing looping. *ERIC Digest*, 123.

Gibbons, G. (2002). *Tell me, tree*. Boston: Little, Brown.

Goodlad, J. (1984). *A place called school*. New York: McGraw Hill.

Goodlad, J., & Anderson, R. H. (1959). *The nongraded elementary school*. New York: Teachers College Press.

Gross, T., & Clemens, S. G. (2002). Painting a tragedy: Young children process the events of September 11. *Young Children, 57*(3), 44-51.

Hall, Z. (2000). *Fall leaves fall*. New York: Scholastic.

Harrington, H. L., Meisels, S. J., McMahon, P., Dichtelmiller, M. L., & Jablon, J. R. (1997). *Observing, documenting, and assessing learning: The work sampling system handbook for teacher educators*. Ann Arbor, MI: Rebus.

Head Start-Public School Transition Demonstration. (1999). Washington, DC: Department of Health and Human Services.

Helm, J., Huebner, A., & Long, B. (2000). Quiltmaking: A perfect project for preschool and primary. *Young Children, 55*(3), 44-49.

Helm, J. H., & Katz, L. G. (2001). *Young investigators: The project approach in the early years*. New York: Teachers College Press.

Henniger, M. L. (2002). *Teaching young children: An introduction* (2nd ed.). Upper Saddle River, NJ: Prentice Hall.

Hughes, E. (2002). Planning meaningful curriculum: A mini story of children and teachers learning together. *Childhood Education, 78*, 134-139.

Iran-Nejad, A., McKeachie, W. J., & Berliner, D. C. (1990). The multisource nature of learning: An introduction. *Review of Educational Research, 60*(4), 509-517.

Jensen, E. (1998). *Teaching with the brain in mind*. Alexandria, VA: Association for Supervision and Curriculum Development.

Kagan, S. L., & Neumann, M. J. (1997). Highlights of the Quality 2000 initiative: Not by chance. *Young Children, 52*(6), 54-62.

Katz, L. G., & Chard, S. C. (2000). *Engaging children's minds: The project approach* (2nd ed.). Stamford, CT: Ablex.

Katz, L., Evangelou, D., & Hartman, J. A. (1990). *The case for mixed-age grouping in early education*. Washington, DC: National Association for the Education of Young Children.

Kohn, A. (2000). *The case against standardized testing: Raising the scores, ruining the schools*. Portsmouth, NH: Heinemann.

Kohn, A. (2001). Fighting the tests: Turning frustration into action. *Young Children, 56*(2), 19-24.

Kovalik, S., & Olsen, K. (1997). *Integrated thematic instruction* (3rd ed.). Kent, WA: Susan Kovalik & Associates.

Kraft-Sayre, M. E., & Pianta, R. C. (2000). *Enhancing the transition to kindergarten: Linking children, families, & schools*. Charlottesville, VA: National Center for Early Development and Learning, Kindergarten Transition Project, University of Virginia.

Kuball, Y. E. (1999). A case for developmental continuity in a bilingual K-2 setting. *Young Children, 54*(3), 74-79.

Lefrancois, G. R. (2001). *Of children: An introduction to child development* (8th ed.). Belmont, CA: Wadsworth.

Leland, C. H., & Kasten, W. C. (2002). Literacy education for the 21st century: It's time to close the factory. *Reading and Writing Quarterly, 18,* 5-15.

Little, T., & Dacus, N. B. (1999). Looping: Moving up with the class. *Educational Leadership, 57*(1), 42-45.

Lubeck, S. (2000, April). *On reassessing the relevance of the child development knowledge base to education: A response.* Paper presented at the Early Education/Child Development SIG, American Educational Research Association, New Orleans, LA.

MacDowell, M. A. (1989). Partnerships: Getting a return on the investment. *Educational Leadership, 47*(2), 8-15.

McIntyre, E., & Kyle, D. (2002). *Nongraded primary programs: Possibilities for improving practice for teachers.* Louisville, KY: University of Louisville.

Maryland State Department of Education. (1998). *Maryland model for school readiness: Fact sheet.* Baltimore: Author.

Miletta, M. M. (1996). *A multiage classroom: Choice and possibility.* Portsmouth, NH: Heinemann.

Miller, B., & Kantrov, I. (Eds.). (1997). *A casebook on school reform.* Portsmouth, NH: Heinemann.

Miller, D. S. (2002). *Are trees alive?* New York: Walker & Company.

Milwaukee Public Schools. (1942). *Curriculum guide for kindergarten-primary.* Milwaukee, WI: Author.

Mitchell, L. S. (1934). *Young geographers.* New York: Bank Street College.

Montgomery, K. (2001). *Authentic assessment: A guide for elementary teachers.* New York: Longman.

Morine-Dershimer, G., & Tenenberg, M. (1992). *Participant perspectives of classroom discourse.* Final Report Executive Summary (NIE G78-0161). Washington, DC: National Institute of Education.

Nash, M. (1997, September 3). Fertile minds. *Time, 152,* 48-56.

National Association for the Education of Young Children. (1988). *Testing young children: Concerns and cautions.* Washington, DC: Author.

National Association of School Psychologists. (2002). *Position statement on ability grouping.*

Bethesda, MD: Author.

National Association of State Boards of Education. (1988). *Right from the start.* Alexandria, VA: Author.

National Center for History in the Schools. (1994). *National standards for history for grades K-4: Expanding children's world in time and space.* Los Angeles: Author.

National Committee on Science Education Standards and Assessment. (1994). *National science education standards: Discussion summary.* Washington, DC: National Research Council.

National Council on Geographic Education. (1994). *Geography for life: National geography standards 1994.* Jacksonville, AL: Author.

National Education Association. (2001). *Issue paper: Class size.* Washington, DC: Author.

National Research Council. (2001). *Eager to learn: Educating our preschoolers.* Washington, DC: National Academy Press.

Nels, E. M. (2000). Academics, literacy, and young children: A plea for a middle ground. *Childhood Education, 76,* 134-140.

New Jersey State Department of Education. (1989). *Guide for teachers, parents, and parent coordinators: Planning for parental involvement in early childhood education.* Trenton, NJ: Author.

Nilsen, B. A. (1997). *Week by week plans for observing and recoding young children.* Albany, NY: Delmar.

Northwest Regional Educational Laboratory. (2001). *School improvement research series: Nongraded primary education.* Portland, OR: Author.

Ohanian, S. (2001). News from the test resistance trail. *Phi Delta Kappan, 82*(5), 363-366.

Ortiz, L. I., & Loughlin, C. E. (1980). *Building curriculum with children: A point of view.* Albuquerque, NM: University of New Mexico.

Paley, V. (1984). *Boys and girls: Superheroes in the doll corner.* Chicago: The University of Chicago Press.

Paley, V. (1988). *Bad guys don't have birthdays: Fantasy play at four.* Chicago: The University of Chicago Press.

Paley, V. (1990). *The boy who would be a helicopter.* Cambridge, MA: Harvard University Press.

Pangrazi, R. P. (2000). *Dynamic physical education for elementary school children* (13th ed.). New York: Prentice Hall.

Parker, S., & Temple, A. (1925). *Unified kindergarten and first-grade teaching.* Boston: Ginn.

Pelo, A., & Davidson, F. (2000). *That's not fair! A teacher's guide to activism with young children.* St. Paul, MN: Redleaf Press.

Perez, B., & Torres-Guzman, M. E. (1995). *Learning in two worlds.* White Plains, NY: Longman.

Piaget, J., & Inhelder, B. (1969). *The psychology of the child*. New York: Basic Books.

Pinnell, G. S, & Fountas, I. C. (1998). *Word matters: Teaching phonics and spelling in the reading/writing classroom*. Portsmouth, NH: Heinemann.

Rebus, Inc. (2001). *The work sampling system*. Ann Arbor, MI: Author.

Rivkin, M. (1995). *The great outdoors: Restoring children's right to play outside*. Washington, DC: National Association for the Education of Young Children.

Rogasky, B. (Ed.). (2001). *Leaf by leaf: Autumn poems*. New York: Scholastic.

SAMPI-Western Michigan University. (2001). *Leadership schools: Progress in implementing whole school reform*. Cambridge, MA: Abt Associates.

Schickedanz, J. A. (1999). *Much more than the ABCs: The early stages of reading and writing*. Washington, DC: National Association for the Education of Young Children.

Schickedanz, J. A., Pergantis, M. L., Kanosky, J., Blaney, A., & Ottiger, J. (1997). *Curriculum in early childhood: A resource guide for preschool and kindergarten teachers*. Boston: Allyn and Bacon.

Scully, P., Howell, J., & Corbey-Scullen, L. (2000). From a bean cake to a classroom kingdom: An idea becomes five weeks of learning. *Young Children, 55*(3), 28-35.

Seefeldt, C., & Barbour, N. (2001). *Early childhood education: An introduction* (4th ed.). Upper Saddle River, NJ: Merrill/Prentice Hall.

Shonkoff, J. P., & Phillips, D. A. (Eds.). (2000). *From neurons to neighborhoods*. Washington, DC: National Academy Press.

Shore, R. (1997). *Rethinking the brain*. New York: Families and Work Institute.

Smith, K. L. (2002). Dancing in the forest. Narrative writing through drama. *Young Children, 57*(2), 90-94.

Spodek, B. (1977). What constitutes worthwhile educational experiences for young children? In B. Spodek (Ed.), *Teaching practices: Reexamining assumptions* (pp. 332-377). Washington, DC: National Association for the Education of Young Children.

St. Louis Association for the Education of Young Children. (1989). *Early childhood transfer form*. St. Louis, MO: Author.

State House Bill 3565 of Oregon. (2001).

Teitel, L., & Abdal-Haqq, I. (2000). *Assessing the impacts of professional development schools*. Washington, DC: American Association of Colleges of Teacher Education.

Terzian, S. (2002). On probation and under pressure: How one 4th-grade class managed high-stakes testing. *Childhood Education, 78*, 282-284.

Thompson, S. (2001). The authentic standards movement and its evil twin. *Phi Delta Kappan, 82*(5), 358-361.

University of Missouri and the Missouri Department of Elementary and Secondary Education. (1991). *Project construct: A framework for curriculum and assessment*. Columbia, MO: Author.

U.S. Department of Education. (1991). *America 2000. An education strategy*. Washington, DC: Author.

Vandergrift, J. A., & Greene, A. L. (1992). Rethinking parent involvement. *Educational Leadership, 50*(1), 57-59.

Vygotsky, L. (1986). *Thought and language* (Rev. ed.). Cambridge, MA: The M.I.T. Press.

Washington, V., & Andrews, J. D. (1999). *Children of 2010*. Washington, DC: National Association for the Education of Young Children.

Weiss, R. P. (2000). Brain-based learning. *Training & Development, 54*(7), 20-24.

Wells, G. (Ed.). (1994). *Changing schools from within: Creating communities of inquiry*. Portsmouth, NH: Heinemann.

Wesson, K. A. (2001). The "Volvo" effect: Questioning standardized tests. *Young Children, 56*(2), 16-18.

Wood, C. (1994). *Yardsticks: Children in the classroom ages 4-14*. Greenfield, MA: Northeast Foundation.

Zimmerman, E., & Zimmerman, L. (2000). Art education and early childhood education: The young child as creator and meaning maker within a community. *Young Children*, 87-92.

CATEGORIZED BIBLIOGRAPHY

ASSESSMENT

Azwell, T., & Schmar, E. (Eds.). (1995). *Report card on report cards: Alternatives to consider.* Portsmouth, NH: Heinemann.

Cohen, D. H., Stern, V., & Balaban, N. (1997). *Observing and recording the behavior of young children* (4th ed.). New York: Teachers College Press.

Curtis, D., & Carter, M. (2000). *The art of awareness: How observation can transform your teaching.* St. Paul, MN: Redleaf Press.

Harrington, H. L., Meisels, S. J., McMahon, P., Dichtelmiller, M. L., & Jablon, J. R. (1997). *Observing, documenting, and assessing learning: The work sampling system handbook for teacher educators.* Ann Arbor, MI: Rebus.

Meisels, S. J., Jablon, J. R., Marsden, D. B., Dichtelmiller, M. L., Dorfman, A. B., & Steele, D. M. (1994). *An overview: The work sampling system.* Ann Arbor, MI: Rebus Planning Associates.

Montgomery, K. (2001). *Authentic assessment: A guide for elementary teachers.* New York: Longman.

Nilsen, B. A. (1997). *Week by week: Plans for observing and recording young children.* Albany, NY: Delmar.

BALANCED LITERACY

Avery, C. (1993). *And with a light touch: Learning about reading, writing, and teaching with first graders.* Portsmouth, NH: Heinemann.

Cunningham, P., & Allington, R. (1999). *Classrooms that work: They can all read and write* (2nd ed.). New York: Longman.

Fountas, I., & Pinnell, G. S. (1996). *Guided reading: Good first teaching for all children.* Portsmouth, NH: Heinemann.

McGee, L., & Richgels, D. (2000). *Literacy's beginnings: Supporting young readers and writers* (3rd ed.). Boston: Allyn and Bacon.

Morrow, L., Tracey, D., Woo, D., & Pressley, M. (1999). Characteristics of exemplary first-grade literacy instruction. *The Reading Teacher, 52*(5), 462-476.

Neuman, S., Copple, C., & Bredekamp, S. (2000). *Learning to read and write: Developmentally appropriate practices for young children.* Washington, DC: National Association for the Education of Young Children.

Oswocki, G. (2001). *Make way for literacy: Teaching the way young children learn.* Portsmouth, NH: Heinemann.

Pinnell, G. S., & Fountas, I. C. (1998). *Word matters: Teaching phonics and spelling in the reading/writing classroom.* Portsmouth, NH: Heinemann.

Schickedanz, J. (1999). *Much more than the ABCs.* Washington, DC: National Association for the Education of Young Children.

BRAIN RESEARCH

Bruer, J. T. (1999). *The myth of the first three years: A new understanding of early brain development and lifelong learning.* New York: Free Press.

Cohen, D. L. (2000). *Good beginnings for all children: From brain research to action: Summary of the forum.* U.S. Office of Education. (ERIC Doc. Reprod. Service No. 423 999)

Diamond, M., & Hopson, J. (1998). *Magic trees of the mind.* New York: Dutton.

Fukuyama, F. (2002). *Our posthuman future.* New York: Farrar, Straus, & Giroux.

Giedd, J. N., Blumenthal, J., Jeffries, N. O., Castellanos, F. X., Liu, H., Zijdenbos, A., Paus, T., Evans, A. C., & Rapoport, J. L. (1999). Brain development during childhood and adolescence: A longitudinal MRI study. *Nature Neuroscience, 2,* 861-863.